D0095864

Advance Praise for GUTS!

"*GUTS!* will leave you shaken, not stirred! It serves up a poignant, powerful recipe for creating leaders who redefine the act of influencing and organizations that reinvent the meaning of business."
—Chip R. Bell, author, *Magnetic Service: The Secrets of
Creating Passionately Devoted Customers*

"This is a genuinely great book! New insights bounce off nearly every page and are guaranteed to propel you into action right away!"
—Tom Morris, author, *If Aristotle Ran General Motors*
and *The Art of Achievement*

"Running a UK high-speed passenger railway is a tough, uncompromising business. . . . *GUTS!* so clearly reminds us that there really is a better way. Kevin and Jackie set out timeless and powerful principles that really DO WORK in business after business."
—Alan Wilson, Managing Director, Midland Mainline Limited, UK

"For years I've told my clients that nobody can teach courage to a leader. The Freibergs may have proved me wrong. *GUTS!* is an exciting presentation of why courage (including passion, boldness, risk, optimism and love) is a must for leaders today—and HOW leaders might beef up their own courage to do what's necessary for competitive success today."
—Oren Harari, Ph.D., author, *The Leadership Secrets of Colin Powell*

"In an age of technology, communication, process and governance, the Freibergs help us discover it's still companies with a heart and soul that really excel!"
—Donald M. Himelfarb, President and COO Franchising, Marketing and
Administration, Dollar Thrifty Automotive Group, Inc.

Also by Kevin and Jackie Freiberg

NUTS!

*Southwest Airlines' Crazy Recipe for
Business and Personal Success*

DAVE —

GUTS!

Companies that blow the doors off business-as-usual

Thanks for making a difference!

CURRENCY

DOUBLEDAY

New York London Toronto Sydney Auckland

KEVIN AND JACKIE FREIBERG

To Dylan,
who is wild at heart and already showing signs of
becoming a gutsy leader.

Dylan, your courage and passion to live life as a daring
adventure inspire us to seize the day!

———————————————

A CURRENCY BOOK
PUBLISHED BY DOUBLEDAY
a division of Random House, Inc.

CURRENCY is a trademark of Random House, Inc., and
DOUBLEDAY is a registered trademark of Random House, Inc.

GUTS! was originally published in hardcover by Currency in January 2004.

Book design by Chris Welch

The Library of Congress has cataloged the hardcover edition of this book as follows:

Freiberg, Kevin, 1958–
   Guts! : companies that blow the doors off business-as-usual / Kevin and
Jackie Freiberg—1st. ed.
      p. cm.
   Includes index.
   1. Leadership. 2. Industrial management. I. Freiberg, Jackie, 1963– II. Title.

HD57.7.1744 2004
658.4'092—dc22   2003062514

ISBN 0-7679-1500-3
Copyright © 2004 by Kevin and Jackie Freiberg
All Rights Reserved

PRINTED IN THE UNITED STATES OF AMERICA

First Edition: January 2004

First Currency Paperback Edition: October 2005
All trademarks are the property of their respective companies.

SPECIAL SALES
Currency Books are available at special discounts for bulk purchases for sales
promotions or premiums. Special editions, including personalized covers, excerpts of
existing books, and corporate imprints, can be created in large quantities for special
needs. For more information, write to Special Markets, Currency Books,
specialmarkets@randomhouse.com

10 9 8 7 6 5 4 3

Contents

TAKE THE *GUTS!* CHALLENGE

Have you ever done something incredibly gutsy at work? Have you ever been willing to risk it all and created extraordinary results in the process?

If not, now is the time.

Go and do something gutsy at your company on your own or with your team. Be unconventional. Create a movement. And then tell us about it. Your story could be highlighted in the paperback edition of *GUTS!*

Go to gutsyleaders.com to take the *GUTS!* CHALLENGE.

Introduction

Back in 1996, we published our own up-close account of one of America's great businesses. We called our book *Nuts! Southwest Airlines' Crazy Recipe for Business and Personal Success*. Much as we admired that legendary airline and its irreverent culture, we were flabbergasted by the book's success. As of 2003, *Nuts!* has sold more than 500,000 copies, and it continues to sell thousands more each month.

Why such interest? Well, it seems that people all over the world crave stories about extraordinary achievers, and Southwest fits the bill. Even in the aftermath of 9/11, with other airlines hammered by financial turbulence, Southwest Airlines soars on wings of success.

Instead of laying off people and cutting flights, it has hired 6,500 new employees and added new routes. Instead of alienating customers, it has generated such loyalty that its passengers often donate unused portions of their tickets to the company and even send in cash. Post-9/11, Southwest is the only major carrier to make a profit every quarter.

Inspired by the Southwest story and its impact on all those who hear it, we set out to find other Southwest-like companies with unusual strategies for attracting talent and ensuring success. *Nuts!* became our passport to amazing organizations, not only those on *Fortune* magazine's various "best" lists, but also companies that may not be on any list at all yet are known as the best within the communities they serve. We discovered organizations full of great people who are turned on, passionate, in love with what they do, and eager to use their skills, gifts, and talents to the fullest. We were determined to pinpoint just why such companies are so unusual.

We confirmed that Southwest Airlines is still outrageously unique and still ingeniously nuts even after all these years, but we discovered something else as well. Many other enterprises, all nutty in their own ways, share an uncommon characteristic with Southwest. They're all run by what we call "gutsy leaders," meaning passionate men and women who don't hesitate to slaughter the sacred cows of convention. We discovered such organizations in fields ranging from software to advertising to the U.S. military. All are led by people with the courage to discard traditional management rules, rituals, and expectations. They are gutsy enough to forge new paths, consistently serve their people first, and pursue a brilliant new way of working, one that we are convinced must dominate business in the decades to come.

Our hope is that this book will help you become more gutsy, too—more engaged, more considerate, more courageous, and most important, a better leader. You may just blow the doors off business as usual in your corner of the world. All it takes is guts.

GUTS!

CHAPTER 1

Gutsy Leaders
Blow the Doors
Off Business-as-
Usual

Gutsy leaders reject the mercenary notion that their employees are nothing more than human resources, akin to capital, fuel, oil, or machine tools, that can be allocated or discarded at will.

Instead, they see their people as individuals with unique gifts and talents, eager to realize their potential. Gutsy leaders aren't afraid of being criticized or even mocked by their competitors. With bravery and vision, they have dismantled fear-based management and replaced it with heart, soul, discipline, loyalty, humor—and long-term

Dare to be Different

> Courage is rightly esteemed the first of human qualities because it is the quality which guarantees all others.
>
> **—WINSTON CHURCHILL**

record profits. By being gutsy leaders, they have led their enterprises to new levels of performance. Exactly why and how gutsy leadership produces such impressive results is the focus of this book.

These leaders teach us that it is absolutely possible to work hard, have fun, love what you do, live your values, and still make lots of money. After six years of observing these leaders in action, we want to spread the word.

Jim Blanchard Has the Guts to Work for His People

Employees work for their boss, right? Not if you work at Synovus Financial. James H. Blanchard, chief executive officer of Synovus, told us repeatedly that he works for his company's people. His mission is to provide whatever they need to thrive, including inspira-

Gutsy leaders have **dismantled fear-based** management and **replaced it with heart, soul, discipline, loyalty, humor**—and long-term **record profits.**

tion, training, resources, and peace of mind. Blanchard's offbeat style is called "servant leadership," a radical concept sweeping many successful businesses today. One of Blanchard's rituals is a weekly meeting with a rock-the-boat agenda. First question at the meeting: "What are the 25 dumbest things we do around here?"

Servant leadership has delivered all sorts of benefits to Synovus's employees—and to its bottom line. For a hint on the employee side,

What's on *Your* Mind?

Jimmy Blanchard, Synovus Financial, doing what he does best, connecting with his people.

consider this: The corporation, employing more than 11,900 people, consistently ranks high on *Fortune*'s list of "the 100 best companies to work for in America." In 1999, it was number one. As for the bottom line, hear this: As of 2002, it had a market capitalization of $71 billion, assets of more than $21 billion, revenues of more than $1.7 billion, and profits of $365 million. Challenged, dedicated employees and rock-solid financials—see a connection there?

Synovus is a financial-services giant based in Columbus, Georgia. It started more than a century ago as a local bank, Columbus Bank

& Trust Company (CB&T), and now encompasses 40 community banks in the Southeast, along with Synovus Insurance, Synovus Mortgage, Synovus Securities, and Synovus Trust.

In addition, Synovus owns more than 80 percent of TSYS, one of the largest payment-processing operations in the United States. CB&T was a pioneer in the credit-card business, in 1959 becoming one of the first banks in the world to issue the cards. Fourteen years later, the company developed a breakthrough software product that permitted electronic access to bank-account data, and began processing other banks' paper, particularly their booming number of credit-card accounts. In addition to its card-processing business, TSYS provides computer-equipment sales and leasing, direct-mail and telemarketing services, and commercial bank-card printing.

If you're not living on the edge, you're taking up too much space.

—ANONYMOUS

As big as it is, Synovus is all about serving small towns, where its community banks offer retail banking, mortgage banking, and credit cards and play a major role in local affairs. It's a name to do business with in more than 250 locations, and the number is growing. Though most of its banking revenue comes from Georgia, the company has been crossing state lines over the last decade, with bank acquisitions in Alabama, Florida, South Carolina, and Tennessee. Synovus has also increased its stake in Internet and investment banking, while gradually diversifying its portfolio, buying auto- and life-insurance companies and Wallace & De Mayo, a leader in the debt-collection field.

In case you were wondering, the name change from Columbus Bank & Trust Company to Synovus came in 1989. "Synovus" is a coined combination of the words "synergy" and "novus," which the company defines as "of superior quality and different from the others listed in the same category."

Roy Spence Has the Guts to Build a City of Ideas

GSD&M, one of the nation's largest advertising agencies and now a subsidiary of the Omnicom Group, is, in reality, in the idea business. In 1971, six graduates from the University of Texas started the organization, based on the premise that big ideas will generate big results. At Idea City, GSD&M's headquarters in Austin, Texas, people develop visionary ideas and strategies that consistently make the client a winner faster than anyone thought possible. As the company's leaders once wrote, "The entrepreneurial—almost primal—drive to create something that was not there before is the simple idea

Roy Spence, President, GSD&M, the visionary behind idea city.
Wyatt McSpadden

that has fueled GSD&M from the start. We didn't know it then, but that idea was to become the essence of our agency. The pursuit and creation of an idea is exhilarating, thrilling, draining, and addictive. It is what we do. It is what drives us."

Roy Spence, president of GSD&M and one of the original six, dreamed of building his own city, and he didn't stop with the dream. Determined to recruit the best creative talent, Spence sought unconventional office space to excite his elite team of fantasy merchants. Genius knocked: He conceived and built Idea City, a far-out complex aimed at sparking creative friction by throwing people together in unexpected ways. Part ancient Greek marketplace, part SoHo atelier, it is carefully designed to smack down conventional wisdom wherever it raises its predictable head.

By not taking itself too seriously, Idea City avoids the pretentiousness that often stifles innovation in other companies. One of the city's two "idea towers" features a huge stuffed cow on a retractable pulley; the other, soundproofed with padded walls, includes a Ping-Pong table, ideal for batting ideas as well as balls back and forth. GSD&M people work in "neighborhoods": a graffiti-adorned Greenwich Village for the copywriters, the financial district for the numbers crunchers.

On the theory that "your butt's connected to your brain" (that is, where you sit shapes what you think), GSD&M has 30 small "war rooms" designed to trigger creativity. The Chili's Bar & Grill war room, for example, is furnished with a booth, menus, and a Tiffany-style lamp hanging over the table. Other rooms are stuffed with assorted branded products and memorabilia from client companies.

No doubt Spence took a risk when he chose to build Idea City in Austin rather than a familiar ad-agency center, such as New York or Los Angeles. Over the years, the risk has paid off in double-digit annual revenue growth. The company now boasts more than

$1 billion in annual billings—from the likes of Southwest Airlines, DreamWorks, Wal-Mart, the U.S. Air Force, Charles Schwab, SBC, and the PGA Tour. GSD&M has been named Southwest Agency of the Year seven times by *AdWeek* magazine. Along with its rivals, the business has been hard-hit by the millennial recession, with a 20 percent drop in revenue in 2002. Undaunted, it increased its staff almost 6 percent to 565.

An occasional economic downturn, though, seems unlikely to dishearten a company with the kind of gutsy idea power GSD&M demonstrated for upscale Doubletree Hotels, a division of Hilton Hotels that is based in Springfield, Oregon.

Rather than the usual industry focus on fancy rooms, swimming pools, and service, the agency convinced its client to develop a new trademark, a chocolate-chip cookie. The cookie, delivered to guests at check-in, became a symbol of the "sweet dreams" and peace of mind that would be Doubletree's chief new selling proposition. The campaign exploded call volume to the chain from 2,000 to 13,000 a day, and helped make Doubletree the fastest-growing U.S. company in the first-class hotel category.

Harry Quadracci Had the Guts to Trust

It takes guts to entrust the business you created to someone else. No one did that more than the late Harry V. Quadracci, founder and president of Quad/Graphics, one of the world's foremost printers, which handles such magazines as *InStyle, National Geographic, Newsweek, People, Time, U.S. News & World Report,* and the prepress business of Condé Nast. It also prints direct-mail pieces, books, retail inserts, and the catalogs Lands' End, Lillian Vernon, and Victoria's Secret. Quadracci believed in "management by walking away," a bet that the more you delegate power, the better your

Harry V. Quadracci, founder Quad/Graphics, based in Pewaukee, Wisconsin.

employees perform. Quadracci fully trusted his people to rise to the occasion to the extent of establishing, over the years, six separate businesses of which employees are part-owners and full-time managers.

The ultimate example of his "management by walking away" is Quad University, an annual event that continues even after Quadracci's sad, accidental death by drowning in July 2002. During the event, all Quad managers take part in a two- to three-day conference hundreds of miles from the Quad/Graphics facilities, leaving rank-and-file employees in charge of everything—scheduling work, running state-of-the-art presses and binders, shipping finished goods, handling crises, and dealing with customers.

Was Quadracci crazy? No, just gutsy.

His baby, Quad/Graphics, was started on a shoestring in 1971 in an abandoned factory in the hamlet of Pewaukee, Wisconsin. He had 11 employees, a rented press, and a borrowed binder. Pewaukee was so far off the beaten printing-industry path that the only jobs it got were those no one else wanted. "We were pretty much known as the company that could do anything," said Bill Deja, the transportation vice president, who epitomizes Quad's "can-do-against-all-odds" culture.

Quadracci couldn't afford to hire experienced people at first, so he took on beginners instead and trained them. As the company prospered, he promoted them and gave them more responsibility. Part of his walking-away agenda was to keep the management structure as flat as possible and to be personally accessible to everyone—but only in those rare circumstances when his people needed his input. The mix of empowered employees and top-management presence gave Quad tremendous flexibility to match its people's do-anything attitude.

In 1977, the corporation had a chance to strut its stuff after landing its first big client, *Newsweek*. That relationship, which lasts to this day, also provided the wherewithal to install state-of-the-art technology, which the company made a tradition. By reason of its private ownership, Quad escaped the merger-and-acquisition mania and debt escalations of the 1980s; banks were happy to lend it the cash it needed to keep upgrading its equipment.

In the last decade, Quad/Graphics has gone global, taking a major stake in an Argentine printer and entering into joint ventures with printers in Brazil and Poland. It also created Parcel/Direct, which provides large-scale shipping services of items such as catalogs. About 11,000 employees do the work and own a substantial chunk of the business, which, as of 2002, enjoyed sales of $1.8 billion, up almost 6 percent from the previous year.

Colleen Barrett Has the Guts to Value Values

To many she is known as the Queen of Hearts. Colleen Barrett, president and chief operating officer of the more than 35,000-person-strong Southwest Airlines, is the highest-ranking woman in the U.S. airline industry. A publicity-shy executive who helped found the company more than 30 years ago in Dallas, Texas, Barrett has been the inspiration behind Southwest's amazing culture. In 1990, she formed Southwest's Culture Committee to preserve and promote the organization's core values, known collectively as "SPIRIT." At the time, culture had nothing like the acceptance it has since gained. From day

Colleen C. Barrett,
President and Chief
Operating Officer,
Southwest Airlines,
based in Dallas, Texas.

one, Barrett perceived the essential role that culture would play in differentiating Southwest Airlines from its industry rivals. Without a doubt, SPIRIT is the superglue that holds it all together.

Thousands of articles have been written about Southwest and its legendary founder Herbert D. Kelleher; they rarely give Barrett the credit she deserves. Her priorities reflect her values, and both are demonstrated in a foregone prize: From 1997 to 2001, Southwest was in the top five of *Fortune*'s list of the "100 best companies to work for in America." In 2002, it didn't make the list. Why? Because Barrett had the guts to remove the company from the competition, saving more than $100,000 worth of employee time that goes into applying for the honor. As she told her people: "It's far more important for each of us to 'walk the talk' than it is to . . . compete on paper with other companies."

Was it a smart call? You decide. In the wake of the 9/11 terrorist attacks, many U.S. airlines were forced to borrow cash, cancel aircraft orders, cut flights, lay off employees, and slash fares. Southwest's story was dramatically different. The airline's people remained strong, dedicated, empathic, united, and highly spirited.

The post-9/11 results speak for themselves:

- Southwest operated at 100 percent of capacity without a single layoff.
- It fully met its obligations to its employee profit-sharing and savings plans, which totaled $197.5 million.
- It inaugurated new routes.
- Its revenue-per-passenger-mile (RPM) share of the U.S. domestic market increased by approximately 25 percent.
- It reported 2002 revenues of more than $5.5 billion, with net income of $241 million and a gross margin of 30.5 percent, compared to 26.02 percent for the industry.

The bold and gutsy leadership that started with Herb Kelleher and Colleen Barrett has created one of the most extraordinary workforces in the United States, along with service, safety, and performance records that blow the competition off the runway.

Barrett helped build the Southwest brand by doing for Southwest people what she expects them to do for Southwest customers—live by the Golden Rule.

Jim Goodnight Has the Guts to Be Extravagant

Is it foolish to pamper people with perks? Not according to Dr. Jim Goodnight, cofounder and chief executive officer of SAS Institute, a

Dr. Jim Goodnight, co-founder and CEO, SAS Institute, based in Cary, North Carolina.

world leader in intelligence-software services. The more you help employees focus better on their work, he believes, the more amazing results they achieve for your organization—and he has the results to prove it.

Goodnight was on the faculty of North Carolina State University in 1976 when he and a friend established a business to market the statistical-analysis software he had devised as a student, and they named it after their product's initials. SAS, which is based in Cary, North Carolina, is still Goodnight's property—he owns two-thirds of the shares, and his cofounder, John Sall, holds the rest.

In the years since, they have transformed their enterprise into the largest private software company in the world, with 9,000 employees, offices in 53 countries, and revenues of more than $1 billion. Until the technology crash of the recent past, the company boasted

24 consecutive years of double-digit revenue growth. That came, in part, because of the corporation's remarkable ability to develop state-of-the-art analytic software for virtually every industry, enabling organizations to mine their databases and use the results to better manage everything from their finances to their human resources to their ability to spot money-laundering transactions. In addition to its technical skills, SAS leads the industry in its wraparound, 24/7 customer service, with an amazing annual renewal rate of 98 percent, and 80 percent of its sales come from those renewals.

Aiding the company's retention rate is an unusual payment arrangement. Unlike most software makers, SAS does not sell product licenses. Its customers pay a yearly license fee of about $50,000 for every 50 users. If a customer doesn't renew its license, its SAS tools and all the applications built on them become inoperative.

Of course, what keeps the products flowing, and the customers content, is a gung-ho, dedicated workforce, which may just be the most important of Jim Goodnight's many achievements. Make employees' lives easier and they will give their all at work! He makes employees' lives a lot easier and much more pleasant. Needless to say, SAS employees give their all at work. In an industry notorious for footloose employees, they stick to SAS like glue, which allows the company to avoid the costly headache of recruiting, training, and assimilating new hires.

According to Jeffrey Pfeffer, a Stanford University professor, "Software companies the size of SAS have to replace more than 1,000 people a year; SAS loses fewer than 100, a difference that saves the company between $60 million and $80 million annually."

Goodnight's gutsy coddle-the-employee policy takes many forms. You're expected to work only 35 hours a week. Your sick days are unlimited and can be used to care for ailing family members. Company specialists can arrange expert help for your aging parents. Your benefits are extended to domestic partners. If you work at headquarters, you can take your preschool kids to one of the two on-site and two off-site Montessori-based childcare centers for $300 a month, meals included.

Each of the 24 buildings on the 250-acre campus has break rooms on every floor stocked with fruit, juices, soda, peanut butter, crackers, and other free snacks. For a full meal, you can choose between two full-service cafeterias, one featuring down-home Southern food, the other offering a broader range of fare. As of 2002, the price of a cafeteria lunch was fixed at $3.50, and you can work all that off in a 54,000-square-foot gym with free personal trainers, an Olympic-size swimming pool, yoga classes, and a dance studio, or on the soccer field, tennis courts, and putting green.

Someone once asked Jim Goodnight if sickrooms could be provided for children who weren't feeling well. "We will never have sickrooms," he answered. "When your children are sick, you need to be at home with them."

Clearly, Goodnight is a man who knows what he wants: employees who are at peace with their families and their lives so they can be devoted to their jobs. He's discovered that gutsy perks pay.

Frederic Holzberger Has the Guts to Care

Beauty is only skin deep, and in our appearance-obsessed culture it took a gutsy beauty-products company to prove it. How? By offering every employee a paid day off to refine his or her inner beauty by working for a local charity of his or her choice. Frederic Holzberger, president and chief executive officer of Fredric's Corporation, a Cincinnati, Ohio, based company that is the exclusive distributor of Aveda Environmental Beauty Products in four midwestern states, believes that no one can have a really full life without being involved in his or her community. And he backed up his conviction with action.

Holzberger attached a caveat to his offer: He wanted a personal account from every employee on how the day went. A year into the experiment, he told us that the program had yielded results far beyond his expectations. Employees reached out and became involved with activities that inspired them, broadened their outlooks, and changed their lives. Holzberger feels that his own life has changed from simply listening to their stories. And we should not forget an

Frederic Holzberger,
President and CEO of
Fredric's Corporation,
based in Cincinnati,
Ohio. *Mark Bowen*

P**eople are never more insecure than when they become obsessed with their fears at the expense of their dreams.**

—NORMAN COUSINS

added benefit: As they shared their experiences with Holzberger, the employees were having high-quality, one-on-one conversations with their chief executive.

Holzberger also devotes himself to his product, the only one he distributes, and to his customers, the beauty salons and retailers that sell that product. Aveda, which is now owned by Estée Lauder, is actually a whole lifestyle system that helps customers become better attuned to the natural world. It uses plant-based products and treatments as well as simple systems to improve their customers' looks and quality of life. Part of the Aveda approach is an emphasis on environmentalism, both in personal lifestyles and in business.

To spread the word about Aveda, Holzberger opened his own 10 stores. At first, 75 percent of the customers had no idea what Aveda was, but the product and presentation were so powerful that the stores were soon generating, as he puts it, "more dollars per square foot than anyone else in the beauty-and-bath category in the malls." Fredric's, as a whole, has been racking up double-digit revenue increases for years, even during economic recessions. In 2002, it boasted sales of more than $36.8 million, up 13 percent from the year before.

In Holzberger, Aveda and its founder, Horst M. Rechelbacher, found their ideal entrepreneur. He is a passionate environmentalist who has also created a truly supportive environment for his employees.

His largely female workforce enjoys fitness facilities, aromatherapy, on-site day care, an organic restaurant, scholarship programs, profit sharing, and Aveda investment opportunities, along with generous bonuses, vacations, and insurance. Few of them ever leave the company.

Holzberger knows that most of his people are performing a delicate balancing act between family, personal passions, and work. He watches, listens, and has the guts to help them in any way he can.

Gutsy Leaders Revealed

In the chapters ahead, you'll read a lot more about all these gutsy leaders and how they've molded their enterprises. You'll also find out about other leaders at other cool companies, some well known, others obscure. We'll tell you about Bon Marché, Planet Honda, Whole Foods Market, USAA, and dozens of other organizations (including one nonprofit) that have inspired us. In identifying companies to write about, we naturally went with our guts. We've worked with some of the businesses featured in this book; others jumped out at us through magazine and newspaper articles; often, one great company would lead us to another. But regardless of how we found them, we have gotten to know them all. All their leaders are different—in fact, each is unique. But they have these things in common:

- They are all pioneers, not followers in their industries.
- They have a record of long-term success and extraordinary business results.
- Whether they are flamboyant or low-key, they are deeply dedicated to inspiring their people to higher levels of engagement and performance.
- They care about their people as individuals, not just "assets" or "resources."
- They are all doing things radical enough to make you say, "That takes guts!"
- What they're doing can be replicated to help other businesses succeed.
- And they all run organizations we'd want to work in ourselves.

All gutsy leaders have vision and the ability to make that vision a reality. They lead by example, both living and imparting the qualities they value and espouse. They seem to naturally inspire others to new levels of achievement and fulfillment. Gutsy leaders care, mentor, challenge, lead, and even love while they work. They know leadership isn't about position or title; it's about influence that flows from believing in something passionately, unwaveringly, and whole-heartedly. People follow gutsy leaders because they want to be part of something special, something different, something they can totally identify with. People don't follow because they have to or because they are expected to. In the organizations we've studied, we've seen remarkable levels of motivation, performance, commitment, and loyalty—and what makes the difference is leadership.

Gutsy leaders are fully engaged, intensely focused, and conta-giously passionate. Winston Churchill said it well: "The key to your impact as a leader is your own sincerity. Before you can inspire others with emotion, you must be swamped with it yourself. Before you can move their tears, your own must flow. To convince them, you must yourself believe."

Gutsy leaders believe. And with good reason. For one, gutsiness pays. Consider this: Had you invested in *Fortune*'s "100 best compa-nies to work for in America" in 1998, then reinvested in the listed businesses every year thereafter, you would have earned 10.6 percent annually. That's nearly double the Standard & Poor 500's 5.7 percent annual return during the same period. So note this: The companies that make the *Fortune* list are invariably great to work for because they're run by gutsy leaders who know what it takes to inspire people toward higher levels of performance and loyalty. Gutsy leaders get results.

The Need for Leaders

We are writing at a moment of enormous turmoil in the business world. The debacles of Arthur Andersen, Enron, Global Crossing, Tyco, and the like have shaken people's faith in the honesty and integrity of large organizations and their executives. We've read about and perhaps even known executives who were driven by greed

GUTS!

and a desire to serve themselves first. As a result, thousands of employees and shareholders are left to deal with incalculable losses. Financial losses, yes, but perhaps more damaging is the loss of faith and trust. All business is bruised, employees are angry, investors are suspicious. Scores of companies have lost the unity, energy, and imagination, to say nothing of the market value, that once sustained them. You can't help wondering: Can these organizations stand up to today's challenges? The blame rests squarely on the shoulders of their failed executives. Never have we needed gutsy leaders more— men and women serving, giving, sharing, inspiring, and delivering.

Go with Your Gut

Gutsy leaders devise smart and purposeful strategies that show respect for people, anticipate their needs, and inspire high performance. They create open, collegial cultures where valuable input is shared and celebrated, whether it comes from the top, bottom, or somewhere in between.

But it is never easy. It takes guts to give the status quo a swift kick in the butt and to venture out to the seemingly lunatic fringe where breakthroughs are born. It takes guts to come down from the ivory tower to listen and talk to people in a human voice. It takes guts to lead with love and trust rather than power and fear. For too many people, it is easy to be hard, and hard to be soft.

To be a gutsy leader, do you have to do every gutsy thing we've written about? Absolutely not! There is no one-size-fits-all prescription for becoming a gutsy leader, and many of the techniques of the leaders we write about would mix about as smoothly as ice cream and hot salsa. But if you can borrow judiciously from the leaders profiled in these pages, applying their ideas to your own talents and personality, you and all the people in your organization will be at an advantage—and much more likely to perform at higher levels.

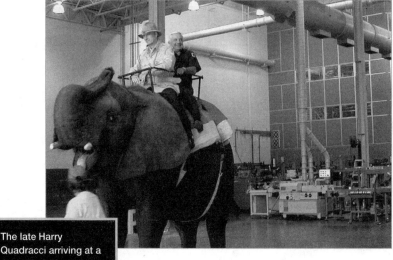

The late Harry Quadracci arriving at a Quad/Graphics party on an elephant.

You have to be gutsy enough to stand up to those who stand in your way. You have to be big enough to admit your mistakes. You have to be vulnerable and say, "I don't know." You have to be humble enough to surround yourself with people smarter and more capable than you. You have to be open and flexible enough to adjust to ever-changing circumstances. You have to ignore those calling for a quick fix or a cut corner. You have to go with your gut, the instinct that feels right and knows best. Do what's right, because it's the right thing to do. That's gutsy leadership.

Different Strokes

Gutsy leaders come in all shapes, sizes, styles, and guises. Jim Goodnight of software giant SAS is the antithesis of Southwest's flamboyant Herb Kelleher. Goodnight is low-key and unassuming; he dislikes public attention, but there is no mistaking his guts and determination in creating a workplace that tries to free people from life's daily distractions. The late Harry Quadracci of Quad/Graphics, on the other hand, often out-Herbed Kelleher, with stunts like arriving at an employee holiday party on an elephant. Quadracci thrived on the bigger, the bolder, the gutsier. In another mold, Jim Blanchard of Synovus is centered, spiritual, evangelical. His quiet integrity seems to inspire everyone in his path.

Only those who dare to fail greatly can ever achieve greatly.

—ROBERT F. KENNEDY

Different leaders, different styles, different strategies—but all are equally gutsy and absolutely unconventional when it comes to creating great places to work and do business.

It was a privilege, an adventure, and a blessing to meet and observe some of the world's gutsiest and most gifted leaders over the five years we spent researching this book. We came to understand that, like great art, gutsy leadership often is derived from indefinable, unspoken, and even unconscious drives and motives. Many of the leaders themselves can't fully explain what they do and how they do it. They are living their values and serving their people based on gut-level instincts. They aren't "analyzing" their methods, "flow-charting" their processes, or "journaling" their styles.

Discovering and experiencing what is behind their success is what motivates us as authors and speakers. There is nothing we relish more than sharing their stories and strategies with interested readers. Our obsession is to share uncommon wisdom, the counterintuitive, the unexpected, the insight that isn't immediately obvious.

We didn't just connect with gutsy chief executives; we spoke in depth with leaders and employees from top to bottom of the companies we studied. Our five years of research produced thousands of pages of material, which we have distilled down to the lessons and illustrations that fill these pages. And our goal is simple: We want you to become a gutsy leader, too.

CHAPTER 2

Gutsy Leaders
Brand Their
Cultures

A few years ago, we drove into the parking lot of Southwest Airlines and saw a young man in front of headquarters holding a sign that read, "Will Work For Peanuts!" He certainly appeared willing to do whatever it took to become a part of Southwest's nutty culture.

On another occasion—this one a U.S. Chamber of Commerce event to launch the publication of our book *Nuts!*—a clever pilot put a placemat with his résumé printed on it at Herb Kelleher's place at the table. His hope? To land a job flying for Southwest.

Not surprisingly, Kelleher noticed, and assured the young man that he would at least get an interview.

Think about it: If people are working that creatively just to get an interview, imagine what they'll do once they're a part of your organization. Even more important in the long term is that companies with what we call branded cultures are places where people both want to work and choose to stay. Having a branded culture is critical to becoming an employer of choice with loyal employees.

If you want to brand your culture, realize that doing so is a long-term process. Culture is not a destination or a program, it's a journey. It's about doing thousands of little things each day because you know they're the right things to do. Is your culture purposeful or accidental? Crafting a culture begins with people, so start by creating a workplace that takes great care of its employees, not just its customers. It's also important to think about your organization's purpose and how its products or services have added value over the years. How would you answer the question, "In what ways are your culture, your products, and your services different from those of your competitors?" Your employees, culture, products, and services are the brand; your people are the ambassadors of the culture. They are a business's most visible and powerful sales and public-relations tools, much more so than any new branding advertising campaign, logo, or slogan.

> High standards of service depend on having staff who are proud of the company. This is why the interests of our people come first. In the end, the long-term interests of the shareholders are actually damaged by giving them superficial short-term priority.
>
> —RICHARD BRANSON

The key point is that you (not an outside organization) need to determine the uniqueness of your business and its culture. Base your branded culture on your ideas and values, not those of consultants. Take a look at Southwest Airlines, which has been a celebrated employer of choice for more than 30 years. Its culture is one that people love to be part of and choose to stay in.

Flying to Freedom

From the very beginning, Southwest aspired to be a unique airline. Its unusual and unwavering goal has been to democratize the skies. By accomplishing this, it has made domestic travel accessible to ordinary people, who now have the freedom and opportunity to do extraordinary things. They can fly to places they never dreamed possible, and employees are able to serve customers in unique ways.

Freedom was part of Southwest's original design. Employees have always been encouraged to apply their special talents to projects, such as driving down costs without compromising safety, service, or flight schedules. Significantly, in 2003, Southwest is the only profitable major airline in the United States. With more than 35,000 employees, it has remained true to its roots. Southwest is an employer of choice, in large measure, because of its branded culture.

Down with "Satisfaction"

Companies with branded cultures—employers of choice—aren't filled with merely "satisfied" employees. Would you be content to create a culture in your workplace that simply satisfies people? We don't think so! Gone are the days when employee satisfaction was the target to hit. We believe employees need to be far more than satisfied. They need to be overwhelmingly enthusiastic about the company. It's time to get rid of those surveys that measure employee satisfaction—or, at the very least, rename them. Think about it: Are satisfied employees likely to go beyond what's required to serve colleagues or customers? Are satisfied employees likely to strive to drive costs out of the business without compromising quality, service, or safety? Are satisfied employees likely to engage with their hearts and minds to come up with innovative approaches to doing business? Are satisfied employees likely to be great ambassadors for your com-

SATISFACTION *(circled with a diagonal slash through it)*

pany, your brand? Instead of a satisfaction survey, we have created an opinion survey and loyalty index that enables our clients to measure all aspects of their culture. The objective here is to create a culture that inspires a healthy level of fanaticism about the company and motivates people to become 100 percent engaged in growing the business. Remember, words are powerful. Consider carefully the words you use and the things you measure.

Loyalty Rules

In today's highly competitive talent market, employee loyalty must be uppermost in the minds of those making hiring decisions. What are you doing to become an employer of choice? In other words, how are you creating a branded culture that inspires loyal, rather than merely satisfied, employees?

We know from experience that when your employees are dedicated to their work and their workplace, they will enthusiastically showcase your brand. And predictably, customers and investors respond whenever a culture becomes so attractive and powerful that it constitutes a brand in and of itself. Avon, for example, has created a culture based on its respect for the women who sell and buy its products; The Body Shop, on its concern for the environment; and Southwest Airlines, on fun and freedom. In other words, it's more than the product or service that generates interest; it's the company's values, as well. The people, the work environment, the values, all contribute to branding the culture. Culture then assumes a life of its own and becomes synonymous with the brand. Culture brands create and reflect emotional, moral, and social bonds among employees, customers, and communities. In some cases, branded cultures transcend the products or services that the companies offer and gain as much fame, if not more, as their products.

Bottom line: A branded culture separates an organization from its competition and places it in a league of its own. Another example is the ice-cream purveyor Ben & Jerry's, which is famous for tithing its revenues to environmental causes. For any customer sympathetic to such issues, spending a few dollars for a Ben & Jerry's product buys more than delicious ice cream; it also makes a small contribution to the health of the planet. A branded culture is, quite simply, value added. A branded culture attracts the "right" kind of talent—people who are drawn to the culture as well as to the work. Since it establishes its own reputation, recruitment is easier because potential hires know much more about the company than just what it produces.

Culture Is a Journey

GSD&M's president and one of its founders, Roy Spence, is more than an advertising executive. He is a dreamer. Describing the conception of Idea City, Spence told us, "When my partners and I started out, we learned everything grassroots. There was no Tom Peters, no one-minute manager. We'd never bought media or created ads. We didn't know how to pay people, or even what titles we should each take on. Instead, we focused on what we did have: common sense and good instincts. From the beginning, we sensed that what a company stands for is as important as what it sells [or] the services it provides. . . . It was just a gut instinct over 30 years ago." Based on that gut instinct, GSD&M has been helping clients brand their cultures ever since.

As Spence said, "Visionary ideas go beyond sales increases and stock quotes. They provide an unassailable base for a marketplace positioning that sets our clients apart from the competition. [They become] unassailable because they reflect the unique culture of the company."

Spence and Herb Kelleher first encountered each other when Spence was creating ads for a congressional candidate whom Kelleher opposed. Spence's man, the underdog, won. The next day, Kelleher called, and the two went out for drinks. Ever since then their companies, GSD&M and Southwest Airlines, have enjoyed an extraordinary partnership.

It was GSD&M that helped take two of the airline's presumed weaknesses—no assigned seats and no meals—and turn them into strengths. It was a heroic cause, a desire to democratize the skies and make flying affordable to everyone, that transformed Southwest's no-frills operation into an airline that gave people on a budget the chance to realize their dream. As you frequently hear on their advertising spots, "You are now free to fly about the country."

Another puzzler that GSD&M solved: How do you get the public to stop littering the roadways of Texas? Laws and regulations weren't working. The agency appealed to the Texas pride of the chief litterers, male pickup drivers between the ages of 18 and 34. The slogan "Don't mess with Texas" was supported by singing commercials performed by well-known Texas entertainers, many of whom donated their time. Visible litter in the state was cut by 72 percent.

One of the agency's most imaginative coups came in response to a plea from SeaWorld, the marine entertainment park, which was just opening. The park wanted to spread word of its existence around the country. GSD&M had a killer idea: paint a Southwest 737 aircraft to look like a killer whale, a notable symbol of SeaWorld. It worked, and Southwest Airlines loved it, too! The plane was unveiled

Headquarters to GSD&M is Idea City in Austin, Texas. *Peter Tata*

as Shamu One at the park's opening, reaping more than $12 million in free publicity. After that, Shamu One (and later, Shamu Two and Shamu Three) carried the SeaWorld message into every major market, helping to make Shamu second only to Mickey Mouse in terms of public awareness.

Idea City, GSD&M's inspirational headquarters building, is the place where it happens, where talented people—"doers and dreamers," in Spence's words—can concentrate on bringing what is only imagined to life for any client that is up for the ride. At Idea City, visionary ideas are just the beginning of an extraordinary journey.

People here are completely engaged in the journey. At Idea City there is no room for in-betweeners. The doers and dreamers are not seeking hollow destinations. While another industry award for the wall is important and symbolizes growth and forward movement, such achievements are not enough. For example, when GSD&M crossed the billion-dollar mark, Spence remembers feeling that destination was empty. When the company won "Agency of the Year" for the first time, that felt hollow, too. Yet there is deep fulfillment, close community, and success for everyone, employees and clients alike. We think that's because these people understand that most of life, and the best of life, is about the journey, not the destination.

What we've learned is that great companies are filled with people who enjoy the journey. Spence said, "At GSD&M we live for the journey. . . . The love of the journey creates that perseverance that takes you through tough times." The destination is a worthwhile motivator, but the journey ought to be the real thrill.

Although Spence does not use the term "branded culture," he clearly employs the concept. From everything we've learned about GSD&M's Idea City, we see that its talented team is, indeed, in the business of helping clients brand their cultures. About culture, Spence told us: "We've always known that what [we] stand for, as individuals and as a company, is as important as the ads we create. [If we] do good work, do right by our clients, . . . our people . . . our neighbors, [and] our community . . . we'll do well. It never has been a trade-off."

GSD&M's culture is rooted in values—freedom and responsibility, community, curiosity, restlessness, winning, and integrity—that the current team of associates as well as the founders fully embrace. When you enter Idea City, you are drawn to the rotunda, where the GSD&M core values are literally etched in stone. Never compromised, these guiding principles come to life through creative people, visionary ideas, and win-win partnerships. Determining how they market to their clients, these values are crucial to understanding GSD&M's uniqueness. In Spence's words, this "is not a company for the tired or timid, the arrogant or the apathetic. We are a curious and restless bunch."

GSD&M's corporate values etched into the atrium floor of Idea City. *Wyatt McSpadden*

Planet Honda's Brand—Fun

Around Union, New Jersey, prospective employees know that Timothy Ciasulli, president and chief executive officer of privately held Planet Honda, has the chutzpah of 18 mortals, is a philosopher with a law degree, and holds four offshore powerboat speed records. He's built an auto dealership that blows the doors off selling cars as usual, with annual revenues of almost $100 million, and he's done it around two core principles: employees for life and customers for life. For both groups, he's accomplished the impossible—he's made car buying fun.

Tim Ciasulli, CEO of Planet Honda based in Union, New Jersey.

When you walk into Planet Honda, it's jumping. Sixteen 40-inch television screens show Hondas on camping trips, winning auto races, maneuvering through a cityscape. (And, as you'll see in Chapter 7, that's just for openers.) Don't know which models would suit your needs best? Visit the tech café and type in answers to a computer's questions about everything from your price range to your taste in features. Press a key, and the computer will come up with the models that match your answers.

In fact, everything at Planet Honda reflects Ciasulli's determination to see his operation from a customer's perspective. He came to that decision the hard way. When he was in his late twenties, he and his brothers owned 13 car franchises, and many of them were a mess. In 1982, J.D. Powers's Customer Satisfaction Index found that three of the Ciasullis' General Motors dealerships were among the 10 worst in the country.

When he started Planet Honda in 1996, Ciasulli made sure that every aspect of the dealership, from sales to service, was designed for the customer's convenience and pleasure. Instead of the usual defensiveness, the customer was to be made to feel welcome, comfortable, and in control of the car-buying experience. The result: customers for life.

To achieve employees for life, Ciasulli has had the guts to make their welfare his personal concern. Is the welfare of your employees one of your top concerns? Upstairs at Planet Honda is a workout room complete with Nautilus equipment, free weights, treadmills, and shower facilities. Ciasulli is one of the few car dealers to establish an ESOP (employee stock ownership plan) for his employees. He told us: "The way I look at it is I have 150 shareholder families that I'm responsible for." Then there's the Wall of Fame, a hallway lined with pictures of employees who have done something heroic to serve a customer or a coworker.

Why would anyone leave? They don't. The attrition rate at Planet Honda is less than 1 percent annually.

At the same time, Ciasulli has high expectations for his people. He strongly emphasizes training. In fact, salespeople spend 25 percent of their time in training. Everyone is cross-trained to help the customer with any question, be it about leasing, finance, parts, or service. There is special training on how to sell to women. After all, women make 85 percent of car-buying decisions. And since Planet Honda's base in New Jersey sits amid one of America's areas of greatest diversity, its employees speak a total of 15 languages.

Ciasulli wants the dealership to be not only a great place to buy cars, but a place where employees can share their gifts and realize their dreams. Planet Honda has done a powerful job of branding itself as an employer of choice.

The Good Life at SAS

Another company that is creating a culture with steadfastly loyal employees is one we met in Chapter 1, SAS Institute. SAS develops highly sophisticated software for business and government. The privately owned SAS doesn't post its earnings and usually shuns publicity. As a result, it has become a quiet giant with one of the most extravagant, employee-friendly cultures in the world.

Though he is the creator and presiding genius of SAS's loyalty culture, CEO Jim Goodnight would much rather talk about his organization's remarkable software than its culture. SAS writes software that rapidly sifts through mountains of information to find patterns and meaning. It's so robust and accurate that the U.S. government uses it to calculate the Consumer Price Index (CPI); Marriott International employs it to manage its massive frequent-visitor program; and both Merck and Pfizer use it in developing new drugs. Of *Fortune's* largest 100 companies, 98 are SAS customers, making it likely that SAS software will touch all of us at some point in our lives, if it hasn't already.

When Goodnight started out, data analysis was simply a scientific means to make sense of vast quantities of information. With SAS leading the way, the science has become much more sophisticated; it can now provide optimum solutions to a given business problem and even help forecast the future. Suddenly, business-intelligence technology has entered the management mainstream.

That has brought competitors flocking, but SAS has thus far more than held its own. The breadth and depth of its product line is unmatched in the industry. So it has for companies in virtually every industry just what they need—or it will make it pronto. Meanwhile, SAS is constantly bringing out new and more advanced software. A recent example: analytical products, with prediction and optimization capacities, for vertical markets such as financial services.

The benefits of bigness wed to innovation showed up after the U.S. Congress passed the Patriot Act in 2001. Giant Bank of America wanted to lead the way in complying with the law's provisions against money laundering, but all the software makers the bank contacted said they would need nine months to develop a system that could spot money-laundering transactions. When the bank asked SAS, the software company was able to deliver a system within 24 hours. That's because it had anticipated the need and developed the product.

> You can dream, create, design, and build the most wonderful place in the world . . . but it requires people to make the dream a reality.
>
> **—WALT DISNEY**

The tougher laws and regulations that followed the widespread accounting scandals of the last few years also proved to be a boon for SAS. They required businesses to provide fuller and more accurate data to regulators, investors, and their boards of directors, and SAS had the business-intelligence software to make that happen.

A key factor in SAS's industry-leading ability to hold on to its customers is its customer-service operation. "They spend a lot of time making sure I'm happy," Irving Tyler, chief information officer at Quaker Chemical, once said. How happy is he? SAS provides Quaker with storage for product sales, customer, purchasing, production, supply-chain, and financial data. Quaker also uses a whole range of SAS management-analysis software, up to and including strategic-performance-management software, which does nothing less than help move the company's performance into closer alignment with its goals.

Customer service is also a major selling point for appliance maker Maytag, typical of the consumer-oriented companies that SAS is increasingly pursuing. "They promised excellent support, and they delivered excellent support," one executive noted.

The software industry crunch has slowed SAS's revenue growth, but the company has had no layoffs and has a big cash trove, on the order of $500 million, which it has used to acquire several software businesses and to boost its sales staff. Its ability to weather the storm is owed, in part, to its private ownership, but more to the skill and dedication of its people.

Life in the Sane Lane

SAS didn't become the Mount Everest of its product category through its high-tech magic alone. Nor did it do so by hiring brilliant engineers, though it has many.

From the very beginning, Goodnight's goal was to create an organization that functioned as a partner with its employees. Knowing that competition for top software designers was fierce, the highly practical Goodnight was determined to have the best talent possible, which he planned to attract and keep by building a company committed to making the life/work balance easier for its people. It is not surprising that SAS has been called "Sanity, Inc." by *Fast Company* magazine. It's a place where employees are encouraged to live a balanced life. They create great software, work on cool projects, make good money, smoke the competition—and go home at 5:00 P.M. In other words, they live life in the sane lane.

Cringing as he remembered a computer-programming job for which he interviewed in the 1960s, before he founded SAS, Goodnight explained why he was so determined to create this culture: "Programmers sat at desk after desk, lined up in row after row . . . no walls, no privacy! It even cost a quarter to get a cup of lousy coffee from a break-room vending machine." Goodnight knew instinctively

Remember: Your most **valuable resources** drive away at the end of **every business day,** and it is **your job** to make sure they are **eager to return** the next morning.

that people's surroundings influence the way they feel and perform. When he started SAS, he understood immediately that the corporation's most valuable resources drive away at the end of every business day, and that it was his job to make sure they would be eager to return the next morning.

Inside the buildings on the SAS campus are offices and workspaces designed to maximize comfort, minimize stress, and increase performance and productivity. On the walls hang more than 3,000 original works of art. SAS is the only business we know of that has an artist in residence. In fact, it has a four-person art group, headed by painter Holly Jones. "I have a hard time explaining my job to outsiders," Jones once told an interviewer. "No one has ever heard of a company employing an artist full-time. And I not only paint, I also buy work from other artists. The culture here celebrates art, and people are always telling me that a certain painting or sculpture has

A life-size chess set on the campus of SAS Institute offers an intellectual diversion to programmers looking for another type of challenge.

become like a friend to them, or that it has triggered their creativity at a key moment. There is a culture of appreciation and mutual support here. It's very gratifying." SAS's culture values creativity. As Goodnight explained recently, "Creativity is extremely important, and I will do anything . . . to get those creative juices flowing."

Family Time

Another significant aspect of SAS's culture that distinguishes it from its competition is Goodnight's dedication to, in his words, making

"it easy for employees to balance their work with their family life."
As we all know, issues often arise that must be dealt with in real
time, not after 5:00 P.M. or on the weekends. SAS meets this universal challenge by providing a host of employee-friendly conveniences.
For example, its on-and-off-site and generously subsidized Montessori daycare program is the largest in North Carolina. In addition to
flexible working hours and unlimited sick days, employees get "kid
days," enabling them to stay home with a feverish child or attend
important events, like class plays. After all, as Goodnight advised,
"You don't get a second chance at the first day of school, the first
play, or the first soccer game. When you have kids, you have to be
there." To encourage families to eat lunch together, SAS equips its
cafeteria with booster seats and high chairs. The SAS seven-hour
workday also helps families spend time together.

A World of Perks

The perks and benefits that Goodnight provides have become legendary, and they're available to all full-time employees in every
department, including landscaping and food service. If you've read
or heard anything at all about the SAS story, then you probably
remember the M&Ms—plain and peanut—delivered to employees
every Wednesday without a hitch, a total of 22.5 tons per year. We
aren't exaggerating when we say the perks are too numerous to list.
Here are a couple of the most impressive.

• Health Care Center

Employees receive free treatment around the clock at the SAS center, but the savings aren't the reason they keep returning. Gale Adcock,
manager of corporate health services, explained: "People will try
something once because it's free. But if they're not receiving quality
care, they won't come back. Our usage numbers alone indicate that

this is a valuable service for our employees." In 2002, the center averaged about 120 visits a day. Approximately 90 percent of the company's employees use it, while at least 50 percent choose the center as their primary source of health care.

The health center is located on the SAS campus, and its 55-member staff includes 11 family-nurse practitioners, three family-practice physicians, two nutritionists, 10 nurses, a psychotherapist, and two physical therapists. Established in 1981, the center logged 36,000 patient visits in 2002, which saved SAS between $500,000 and $1 million in time that employees weren't away from work. Additional savings not included in the calculation are productivity gains and lower treatment costs because employees seek treatment early. On average, an SAS employee can have a medical appointment in about 30 minutes, only four minutes of which is spent waiting for the physician. How does that compare to your last visit to your doctor's office? SAS estimates that a visit to an off-campus doctor typically takes about three hours away from work.

• Work-Life Department

Dianne Fuqua created this department in 1991 when she sensed that a number of SAS employees were dealing with elder-care issues. Since then, the department has grown from one to seven full-time employees who are dedicated to helping employees balance work and family. This is how Dianne describes her organization: "We make it convenient and easier for employees to get the resources they need to get things done, whether it's help with an elderly relative, preparing for retirement, or even adopting a child." The department also offers help with issues such as financial aid, problematic youngsters, or getting teenagers ready for college. In addition, financial advice is available free of charge to help employees set up retirement plans, prepare for college tuition, or simply to plan for the future.

About SAS's extraordinary culture, Goodnight once stated: "It's

This fountain creates a parklike setting in the center of the SAS 250-acre campus.

the way it must be. [I want] an environment where people enjoy working, where ideas pour out of their heads and onto a computer screen." The campus, the culture, the art, the design, the software, and all the benefits have become the brand. Even at company operations away from Cary, employees enjoy the advantages of that culture in a carefully selected environment. In Marlow, England, for example, the SAS office occupies the onetime estate of a nineteenth-century tea merchant, Lord Davonport; in France, the office is in a seventeenth-century chateau.

SAS is a celebrated employer of choice, with a culture designed to encourage employees to live full lives as they produce innovative and flawless software.

One of the twenty-four office buildings on the SAS campus. At SAS Institute, most employees have private offices.

Work, Work, Work

As impressive as SAS's perks are, they do not explain Goodnight's success in creating a loyal culture. People don't stay for the M&Ms or the fitness center. They stay because they love their work. Kathy Passarella, who came to SAS from Bell Labs and currently trains new research-and-development employees, explained that "because we are given so much support for our outside lives, when we're here the work becomes our sole focus. . . . When you walk down the halls, it's rare that you hear people talking about anything but work. This culture makes us all want to give back, to work hard, and [to] support each other. Be yourself, do your job, support your colleagues, have a little fun. That's what it's all about."

Jeff Polzin, a systems developer with SAS for 18 years, thought he wanted a change, so he went to work for Cisco Systems. Nine months later, he was back at SAS, once again reveling in this culture of work. "Technical procedures that took hours at Cisco typically took minutes at SAS," he said. "I came back, and in three weeks at SAS, [I] did more than I did in nine months at Cisco."

When we had lunch with two SAS developers, they told us, "We're not here because of the incredible perks. We're here because we get an opportunity to develop exotic software. But, if another company gave us a similar offer to work on cool software, it would be hard to leave SAS because of all the benefits we can take advantage of."

No matter whom we talked with—people who maintained the grounds, taught at a Montessori center, checked people in at the health center, or worked on highly sophisticated intelligence software—SAS workers were passionate about the work they do.

A Branded Culture Pays

The success of SAS's branded culture is reflected in the numbers. In 2002, SAS recorded sales of more than $1 billion—four times its revenues of a decade earlier. The company now employs 9,000 people worldwide, up from 1,900 five years ago, and serves more than 40,000 customers in 118 countries.

Despite conventional wisdom that the only way to attract and keep top talent in the software business is to offer stock options and sky-high salaries, SAS offers no stock, and its salaries are considered "competitive." However, it offers profit sharing—an average of 15 percent of salary annually for the past 25 years. In 2002, its turnover rate was 3.7 percent, compared to an average 25 percent in most other high-tech organizations. In its entire history, SAS's turnover has never risen above 5 percent. Since replacing an employee usually costs about 1.5 times his or her salary, SAS saves an estimated $70 million a year in recruitment and training—an amount that allows the corporation to spend an additional $12,500 per employee on benefits. Unsurprisingly, SAS receives an average of 200 résumés for every job opening.

How did Goodnight brand his culture in this way? For one, he paid attention to his people's needs. When SAS was still a start-up, he realized that some of his most talented employees were women who were having children, then opting to stay at home. Hoping to get them back, he decided to provide daycare. The idea was successful, and the number of new moms who returned to work increased dramatically. Goodnight continued to add perks and benefits designed to help women balance work and family, and today 51 percent of the company's managers are female.

To keep the culture fresh and evolving, employees are surveyed every year, and their comments and suggestions go directly to Goodnight and his executive team. In addition, a benefits group made up of representatives from across the organization meets monthly to discuss proposed new perks. They ask three questions:

- Is the benefit in sync with SAS's culture?
- Would it serve a significant number of employees?
- Would it be cost-accountable—that is, would its perceived value be at least as high as its actual cost?

For a benefit to be adopted, it must meet all three criteria.

Goodnight considers the human-resources department the guardian of SAS's branded culture, and its role has expanded over the last several years. He explained, "HR helps us analyze what our competitors are doing in terms of benefits. We want to stay one step ahead of everyone else. HR also makes sure we don't get complacent about hiring. Just because good people often come to us doesn't mean we shouldn't go looking for great talent. HR also tracks employee satisfaction and turnover. It is the nerve center for measuring the success of our culture in meeting employees' needs."

Of course, human resources uses SAS's own data-analysis software to reveal patterns or trends that deserve attention. "We noticed that we [had] . . . turnover in employees who had been here five to eight years," Goodnight said. "It's a particularly vulnerable group. Five years is a point when talented employees tend to get restless. Ironically, that's often the same point when they perform better than ever. We did some competitive-salary analysis and discovered we were a little below the average for this group. So we corrected their pay."

In this way, SAS has developed a remarkably responsive culture that discerns employees' wants and needs even before the employees articulate them.

Jeffrey Chambers, SAS's vice president of human resources, explained: "To attract people, we need a strong employment brand. This means that when talented people hear our name they have some instant associations—that SAS is a place that respects and trusts its people, that has superlative benefits, that celebrates diversity and creativity. That's why culture branding is so crucial."

The SAS culture offers stimulating and challenging work, an accepting and enriching environment, and respect for family and personal time. As a result, it has a workforce of unmatched loyalty. SAS blows the doors off employee loyalty as usual.

Cultures Can Change

You may be thinking that surely SAS is unique—a private company run by a generous visionary who had, from the very beginning, the guts and freedom to brand his culture in a way no one else could. In contrast, your own company may be a public corporation beholden to people with neither the interest nor the financial freedom to create an SAS-like workplace. In fact, this may explain why your organization is in trouble. The notion that culture change can't happen is a myth, so don't believe it. There's no question that a failing culture can recover, but the task requires determination, persistence, and guts. We offer two unusual examples. One is the National Tax Compliance Group at Ernst & Young; the other is Bon Marché, the once-floundering clothing chain that now is part of Federated Department Stores.

Works in Progress

In the spring of 1999, the leaders of Ernst & Young's National Tax Compliance Group decided they wanted their practice to be "different." Considered by some to be unorthodox (by us, gutsy), they created a work environment in which people could be themselves without compromising their professionalism. The goal was for people to have fun, even as they performed highly technical work under strict deadlines. National Tax Compliance set out to create a place where everyone cared about one another and loved to come to work.

The motive for the change was simple. Alan Kline and Eric Wolf, who headed the organization, knew that if they were to remain an employer of choice practicing world class tax-compliance, they had to attract and keep the world's finest, most effective tax professionals. But before Kline and Wolf made any decisions, they researched the concept of culture change and found Gallup studies showing

Eric Wolf, Jim Godfrey, and Alan Kline, the gutsy leaders who set out to change the culture at Ernst & Young, National Tax Compliance Group.

that "happy" employees are not only more productive but tend to stay with their employers longer. Employees, too, recognize that they will, in turn, reap the rewards of a growing and prospering organization. For the gutsy leaders at National Tax Compliance, culture change was a good business decision. Studies show that "happy" employees are more productive and more loyal.

Changing an organization's culture is no small task, and the stakes were high. The E&Y division of which National Tax Compliance is a part, along with the law group, had sales in 2002 of $3.4 billion, representing almost a third of the firm's total. "Where do we begin, what do we change, and how do we measure it?" were just a few of the initial questions. The leaders of National Tax Compliance

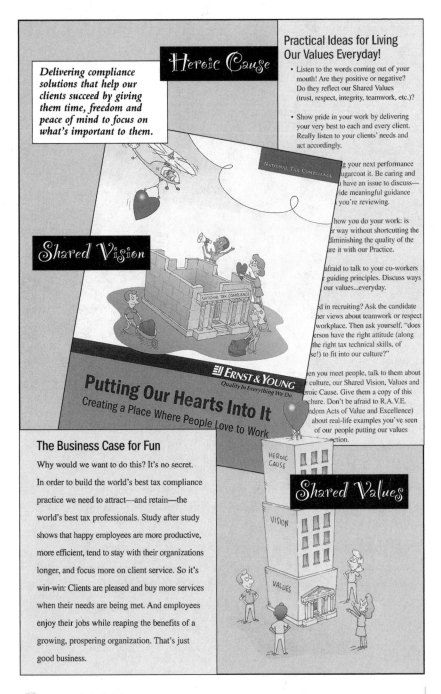

Heroic Cause

Delivering compliance solutions that help our clients succeed by giving them time, freedom and peace of mind to focus on what's important to them.

Practical Ideas for Living Our Values Everyday!

- Listen to the words coming out of your mouth! Are they positive or negative? Do they reflect our Shared Values (trust, respect, integrity, teamwork, etc.)?

- Show pride in your work by delivering your very best to each and every client. Really listen to your clients' needs and act accordingly.

g your next performance
ugarcoat it. Be caring and
have an issue to discuss—
ide meaningful guidance
you're reviewing.

how you do your work: is
r way without shortcutting the
liminishing the quality of the
re it with our Practice.

afraid to talk to your co-workers
r guiding principles. Discuss ways
our values...everyday.

d in recruiting? Ask the candidate
her views about teamwork or respect
workplace. Then ask yourself, "does
erson have the right attitude (along
the right tax technical skills, of
se!) to fit into our culture?"

en you meet people, talk to them about
culture, our Shared Vision, Values and
eroic Cause. Give them a copy of this
chure. Don't be afraid to R.A.V.E.
ndom Acts of Value and Excellence)
about real-life examples you've seen
of our people putting our values
ction.

Shared Vision

National Tax Compliance

ERNST & YOUNG
Quality In Everything We Do

Putting Our Hearts Into It
Creating a Place Where People Love to Work

Shared Values

The Business Case for Fun

Why would we want to do this? It's no secret. In order to build the world's best tax compliance practice we need to attract—and retain—the world's best tax professionals. Study after study shows that happy employees are more productive, more efficient, tend to stay with their organizations longer, and focus more on client service. So it's win-win: Clients are pleased and buy more services when their needs are being met. And employees enjoy their jobs while reaping the benefits of a growing, prospering organization. That's just good business.

searched for a model of a branded culture that seemed right, and they found it in Southwest Airlines. So, in April of 1999, they asked us to help them create a "Place Where People Love to Work."

The journey was engaging and the goal was lofty: "to involve as many people as possible and to give everyone in the practice an opportunity to have their ideas heard." To begin the journey, many of the partners and other key players spent a full day off-site exploring the heroism in what tax compliance does and what value they provide for clients. The full day was followed by a tour around the system. Alan Kline said, "It wasn't logistically possible to bring all our people to one location, so instead we went to them. We asked people in all areas of the practice for their input on the heroism in their work." Yes, it took a few months. It was time-consuming, exhausting, and at some points it felt redundant. But in the end, it was truly exhilarating. The National Tax Compliance team (and it really was a large group effort) identified and articulated a shared set of values, a vision, and a heroic cause that everyone had owernship in. And with only a few years of the process behind them, the practice has incorporated these guiding principles into all aspects of its operations, including recruitment, orientation, performance management, and workspace design. In 2002, a Gallup survey that measures employees' engagement levels was 3.83, up from 3.75 in 2001 (based on a four-point scale, with 4 being highest).

Like all serious culture changes, including that of E&Y's Tax Compliance Group, the following company is a work in progress.

Hard Times at the Bon

Back in 1890, when Edward and Josephine Nordhoff opened their first shop on the outskirts of Seattle, Washington, they named it after the legendary Paris emporium Au Bon Marché, or "good buy," the first modern department store. Edward hoped that their shop would meet the customer-service standards he had so admired during a stay in Paris. The couple invested their entire savings, $1,200, in inventory, and Josephine learned Chinook in order to serve their Eskimo customers.

The Bon, as it came to be known, was a modest success, but the economic panic of the middle 1890s threatened to close down the business. Then Edward had an idea. At the time, Seattle stores made change only to the nearest nickel. Returning from a trip east, Edward brought back sacks of pennies, and hard-hit customers walked long distances to get their change in pennies at The Bon.

In 1896, The Bon moved to downtown Seattle and began a long period of spectacular growth. Josephine carried on the customer-service tradition after Edward's death in 1899, and she became one of Seattle's most generous and beloved citizens, supporting charities and such employee-related goals as the eight-hour workday. In a rare tribute, all of Seattle's major retail establishments closed their doors on the day of her funeral.

The Bon's success led eventually to a chain of 49 outlets scattered around the Northwest, with 6,900 employees. Some stores offered a full line of clothing and home products, others one or the other. The chain was bought by Federated, which also owns Bloomingdale's and Macy's, in 1988, and, for a time, seemed to prosper. Then hard times hit.

As of 1988, sales were flat and morale was low, with a high employee-turnover rate. The company's employees had as much regard for their employer as The Bon had for them—virtually none. Customer services, the hallmark of the original store, had deteriorated. Managers at Federated worried that the chain could not survive.

"There's no doubt we were in big trouble," said Dan Edelman, The Bon's chairman and chief executive. "You only had to walk around one of our stores to feel the lack of energy. Department stores are part theater; they need life, sparkle, vibrancy, *joie de vivre*. Our people weren't happy. There was no sense of community. In fact, there was an 'us-versus-them' mentality. . . . It didn't take me long to realize that the problem was our culture—it wasn't vibrant, vital, or serving our people well." Edelman knew he could not expect instant results from a change in culture. But still, he said, "I set out to change it."

First, Edelman surveyed employees. The results confirmed what he already suspected: People felt the company was autocratic, inflexible, and unresponsive to their needs. The culture, such as it was, was based on slogans, pep talks, and a few inexpensive and unimpressive perks. Edicts came from on high; there was little follow-through and even less buy-in. Employees were wary, if not already jaded. Edelman was confronting a culture in crisis.

He trusted his gut and decided to turn around the organization—that is, to make the corporation work for its people, a strategy that many managers would consider softheaded. But with Edelman's far-reaching vision, which included a new name for the company, the BonLife program was born.

As he explained, "The goal was simple: to make The Bon Marché the best place to work and the best place to shop. Reaching the goal wasn't simple. It took methodical planning and execution. We didn't want to impose any of this change. In fact, we didn't even know what form BonLife would take, other than the broad outline."

The Turning Point

Edelman enlisted Edward Cooney, senior vice president of human resources. Cooney's view of the process is interesting: "While we were still in the early stages of formulating BonLife, I went to a large marketing-department meeting. The subject was the need to put more focus on our brand—make it stand for fun, liveliness, and caring for customers. I said it wouldn't work. There was a silence in the room, and then someone asked me why. I said because we're not taking care of our people, so how can we ask them to take care of customers? If you're not taking care of your people, how can you expect them to take care of the customer?

"We did some brainstorming and came up with categories . . . to reshape the culture. These included people, service, benefits, morale, hiring, measuring, and responding. I still have some of my handwritten notes from this meeting, and consider it an early milestone in BonLife's evolution."

Excited by the initial reaction, The Bon's managers decided to call the new culture BonLife and introduce it to the entire organization in a way that reflected what the new culture stood for. The goal was to get people's attention by demonstrating how the culture had to shift—and why the effort needed everyone's participation.

A Change of Style

"We have a monthly meeting where we bring together anywhere from 300 to 500 people from across the company," Cooney explained. "It's part pep rally, part update, part networking and connecting. It had always been pretty formal . . . with podiums and everyone dressed in suits and dresses. At the monthly meeting [at which] we introduced BonLife, Dan Edelman and our president did their spiel from the podium as usual. Then we darkened the room and put on a videotape. When the tape was over, the lights came up, and there was Dan with the whole executive committee—dressed in casual clothes. There was an audible gasp. Dan cracked a joke and laughter filled the room. The podium was gone, too. They sat in chairs in a semicircle."

Cooney continued: "Then we displayed the e-mail message that had been sent out to everyone in the company that day. It announced BonLife, mentioned the different categories we would be working on, and invited people to participate. We then launched into a no-holds-barred discussion of the obstacles we faced in changing our culture."

The New Deal

BonLife evolved as a social contract in which management and employees agreed to address problems together. Edelman and Cooney knew that the company would succeed only if it evolved organi-

"**People** want to be **part of the solution,** part of something **positive**. It's up to management to **tap into** that **reservoir of goodwill and caring energy.**"

cally, with input and buy-in from everyone. They had to offer tangible benefits that were tailored to the needs of their people, and they did.

Cooney smiled as he remembered what happened next: "We asked for volunteers to join teams that would work on the various aspects of BonLife. Almost immediately, we had more than 140 volunteers. It was electric, what happened in that room. It touched me in a way few things in my career have. Then we put out the call to the rest of the company, and within 48 hours we had over 200 more volunteers. . . . [It] really showed me that people want to be part of the solution, part of something positive. It's up to management to tap into that reservoir of goodwill and caring energy."

The company set up six teams, each charged with developing a set of cultural values, and they made specific recommendations reflecting those values. Ideally, the values should drive the specifics, which is what happened. In this way, the process flowed naturally from philosophy to practicality.

"One of the values was helping people balance their work and personal lives, and the team looked at telecommuting," Cooney said. "Based on their recommendations, we invested significant sums in replacing our desktops with docking stations so that our people [could] . . . stay home and take care of a sick child or go to a school event, and still get work done. This is what our people want: less stress and pressure. You know, stress is a funny thing. On the job, it can be healthy . . . [push] us to do our best work. But what BonLife aims to minimize is the stress surrounding the job—the challenge of integrating life and work."

As BonLife took shape, more benefits were offered in response to employees' input, including flextime, bonuses, a casual dress code, and pets on the job. Morning coffee and pastry were added, as were subject-specific breakfast chats and outdoor barbecues on Puget Sound.

A Risk Pays Off

Bon Marché risked everything when it committed itself to employees over customers, but it worked. Similarly, Southwest Airlines boldly claims that their employees come first, before their customers. And SAS, too, is without a doubt an employee-first culture. Goodnight told us, "It sounds simplistic, but I think history has shown that when you take care of your employees, they, in turn, will take care of the customer." The Bon's Edelman expressed his passion about employees-first this way: "I think putting the customer before your people is the wrong way to go. That may sound like business heresy, but think about it. The customer spends at most a couple of hours a week in a Bon store; our people spend eight hours a day there. And it's our people who are the primary communicators of our culture, the living embodiment of our culture brand. Slogans, design, quality merchandise, and marketing all play key roles, of course, but it's service that sets you apart in this business. Our customer-satisfaction levels have skyrocketed since we began BonLife. That's because our people feel part of a caring community and, as a result, they're doing a better job." The quality of service extended to customers is a direct reflection of the quality given to employees. When you put employees first, they will put the customer first.

In its early days, BonLife met with resistance from high-level executives. Edelman met this challenge swiftly and with admirable savvy. "I took our entire executive committee off-site for a couple of days to really hash the whole process through. I wanted them to understand that they were a part of BonLife, and that it was in their self-interest to support it. The retreat was facilitated and directed by professionals. It was incredibly helpful. Now, every six months we repeat what we call our '10,000-mile checkup.' Cultural change is a process that never ends. We are all human, we all have a tendency to be less than perfect, to slip back into some old behaviors. It is so important to stay focused on the positive, on moving forward, not carping and second-guessing and playing the blame game."

The results prove Edelman's philosophy and actions to have been wise. As recently as 1999, Bon Marché languished in sixth place in the customer-service competition within Federated Department Stores. By 2002, it had advanced to first place. In addition, the number of open jobs has dropped 75 percent, and the rare openings are snapped up within days, not months. Many more management positions are being filled internally. As for sales, they reached more than $1 billion in 2002.

The BonPromise to Customers

Of course it took more than happy employees to achieve these numbers. At the same time it was branding an employee-first culture, BonLife organized focus groups to define exactly what customers wanted. After analyzing the data, managers made the BonPromise to customers: "We understand you have a style that's all your own. You can trust The Bon Marché for the quality, style, selection, and service you deserve for yourself and your home, to look good and feel right."

Just because the **brand** is **successfully established,** it is a mistake to take it for granted. It has to be **constantly renewed, nurtured, and nourished**.

For customers, the BonPromise is the heart and backbone of the store's newly branded culture. Every time a customer steps into a Bon Marché, he or she enters a world committed to superlative service, cleanliness, order, smiling faces, and material wonders—in short, the good life as well as the good deal.

Throughout the gestation period of its new initiatives, the company communicated its brand aggressively, using e-mail, shows, teams, large meetings, and small informal chats to keep employees involved and up-to-date. Judging by customer reaction, the BonLife and the BonPromise also proved to be effective as the basis of advertising and marketing campaigns.

"This company has really turned itself around," said Sharon Carroll, who started with The Bon in 1990, left, and returned in 1998. "I really enjoy coming to work now; it isn't such a pressure cooker. I feel valued for my contributions, which wasn't the case when I worked here before. It wasn't the kind of atmosphere where you would call up the CEO and offer an idea. Now I feel absolutely comfortable e-mailing Dan Edelman. In fact, he invites us to."

A Journey Together

Edelman and BonLife's culture in general celebrate open communication among employees at all levels. Not only does Edelman solicit and read e-mail from his people, he acts on many of the suggestions. Edelman wants to know "if people are unhappy. . . . If they're happy, I want to hear about that, too. Most of all, I want to build a culture based on open communication and shared goals." Edelman is known for prowling store aisles, offering support and encouragement, and discussing informally the countless details that add up to the pleasurable shopping experiences that customers report.

Candor is a crucial value in BonLife, and it fosters a policy of tending to problems immediately rather than denying them. During one large sale, for example, the registers and terminals at four stores didn't function properly, causing customers to wait in long lines. The salespeople were as upset as the customers. Edelman sent a letter to every associate at those four stores in which he assumed responsibility for the mess, apologized for letting people down, and thanked them for rising to the occasion.

Defining a culture and delivering it have clearly been successful for Bon Marché. In Edelman's words, "Few companies are able to say they are truly the premier company in their marketplace. We can. The reason is that we are focused on realizing and living out our culture—celebrating the good life in the Northwest. BonLife has enabled us to hire, develop, motivate, and retain very talented people. BonLife reflects our corporate philosophy [of] keeping all our business practices good, simple, casual, and real. We work hard—but we also work hard at balance, too. We enjoy our lives in and out of the company."

Still, Edelman cautions, just because the brand is successfully established, it is a mistake to take it for granted. It has to be constantly renewed, nurtured, and nourished. "Culture is not about reaching a fixed goal. That's how companies grow stale; they reach a goal and then deflate. Culture is living, breathing, continually adapting. When I'm asked where I want BonLife to end up, I answer that I don't know. How could I? I'm not making the rules, just trying to provide a little guidance and inspiration. This company is a community and we're all on a wonderful journey together."

Bon Marché has reinvented itself and become an organization that enhances everyone who comes into contact with it. Now Bon Marché provides thousands of people with an aura of the tangible and intangible aspects of the "good life." Having the courage to convert a stale culture into an exhilarating brand has produced a retail business with a moral purpose that excites managers, inspires employees, delights customers, and enriches the communities it serves.

A culture of caring for employees will bind them to their organization far more strongly than such conventional perks as stock options, lofty salaries, or long vacations. But caring is only the first step toward making employees productive partners in the enterprise. The next step is giving them a sense that they are actually owners of the business—the topic of our next chapter.

Here are questions to ask yourself, but don't read them unless you are truly committed to the hard work that building a branded culture requires.

✓ **Mission, vision, and values:** Fundamentally, why do we, as a business, exist? How do we want our employees, customers, suppliers, and shareholders to perceive us? When the workday is over, what do we want our employees to think, feel, and say about us? How do we want our customers and suppliers to experience us? When people invest time, talent, and money in us, what do we want them to receive in return? What values are driving our business? What is not negotiable?

✓ **Driving force:** Is our culture sales-oriented, customer-centric, product-driven, or is it managed by the numbers? Do we have a short-term, quarterly focus, or do we take the long view?

✓ **Design and structure:** Is our organizational structure bureaucratic and hierarchical or lean and flat? Do we communicate via first names? Is our style of relating to each other rigid and formal or relaxed and informal? What do our answers say about how much we trust one another? Are people in our company motivated by fear or do they feel secure?

✓ **Performance:** Are we laser-clear about how our strategies and goals support the company's mission and vision?

Are we disciplined at operations? Are we adept at measuring performance and encouraging accountability? Are we straight-forward when discussing performance, or do we hint and hope instead of reporting the facts? How do we react when we miss targets, deadlines, and have to do redos? Is our culture perceived to be a high-functioning meritocracy or one where a sense of entitlement prevails?

✓ **Control:** How do we make decisions within our culture? How do our control systems reflect our beliefs and assumptions? Do we trust people to act ethically, or have we set up an inordinate number of controls? Do our systems and processes facilitate or impede performance?

✓ **Nature of the work:** Is the nature of our work exciting and compelling? Will it make a difference in people's lives? Is anyone in our organization working on a project that will be meaningless in four years? Do we offer each other the freedom to reframe or redefine pointless projects into work that is interesting, challenging, and provocative?

✓ **Relationships:** Does our culture encourage and support close friendships at work? Do we value and respect the concept of family? Do we encourage social activities, such as those sponsored by Frederic's, GSD&M, SAS, Southwest Airlines, and Synovus?

✓ **Leadership expectations:** Are our expectations for leaders in our company clearly laid out? Does our culture encourage people to tell their leaders exactly what they think and feel? Are our leaders committed to and passionate about helping others become successful, or are they too self-involved? Are our leadership expectations available for the whole company to consider, as they are at Synovus?

✓ **Focus on the whole person:** Do we feel comfortable discussing our personal lives and family issues at work? Does the culture encourage and support our interests outside of work? Do our benefits reflect the company's concern that we achieve a comfortable balance between work and the rest of our lives? Do we have a department dedicated to work/life issues? Along those lines, do we provide on-site child care and medical facilities, as SAS and Quad/Graphics do? Do we encourage our people to design individual plans for their personal and professional development, based on their own unique proficiencies and interests, as Planet Honda and Synovus do?

✓ **Rewards and punishments:** What conduct and activities does our organization reward and punish? Are those behaviors consistent with the culture we want, or does the reward system reveal discrepancies between our actual culture and the one we'd like to have, or even believe we have? Does the reward-punishment system contradict the values we espouse? For example, if we champion teamwork, do our incentives promote collaboration or inadvertently endorse competition? If we urge people to take risks in order to produce innovative services and products, how do we react when intelligent and good-faith efforts fail? How do we respond to mistakes? In its soul, is ours a culture that blames or forgives?

✓ **Heroes:** Who become heroes in our organization? What do they do or represent to earn that status? Why are they worth emulating? Do we reward the people who provide exceptional service, who unselfishly support their coworkers, who take risks and push limits in order to create breakthroughs? Do they become the subjects of memorable and legendary stories that capture the spirit of the company's culture?

✓ **Value of stories and legends as teaching tools:** Do we pursue illustrative stories about our organization that link us to its origins and inspire us to progress into the future with traditions that represent the best business we can be? Do we take advantage of every (or almost every) teachable moment? Are we accomplished at using stories as teaching tools that help people understand and integrate the conduct and attitudes we value? Do our stories awaken feelings of institutional pride in both employees and customers? Do our leaders have "eureka" moments like those experienced by Herb Kelleher and Rollin King when they sketched their promising vision for Southwest Airlines on a cocktail napkin? Put another way, do we have stories that epitomize the soul of our culture?

✓ **Physical environment:** What does the physical layout of our company reveal about its character and personality? How are our feelings about rank, class, or status communicated by the way we have allocated the space? What do the wall decorations convey about our values and priorities? Do we hang photos of former employees or posters of old ads, the way Southwest Airlines does? Are there ugly air ducts and intrusive pipes that could easily be painted bright colors, as Quad/Graphics does?

Considering these questions, examine what your company already provides and what it's missing. Now here are some ideas for achieving a branded culture that we have learned from experience.

A glimpse of the photo album–like hallways at Southwest Airlines General Offices at Dallas, Love Field.

✓ **Changing your behavior:** A company's culture is nothing more or less than the result of the choices and behaviors made by its people. Personal change most often precedes organizational change. Changing behavior, which means your own as well as everyone else's, is the only way to change a culture. One can determine quite a bit about a company's culture and character by its priorities. Based on how you answered the above questions, how must you change your organization in order to create the culture you want? Start today by creating an action plan.

✓ **Managing the business:** Your business is its culture. The two are inextricably entwined; thus, attempting to divide them in order to treat culture as a collateral issue is an error and will fail. The character and quality of your culture will determine how work is done; how the company interacts with its employees, customers, and partners, as well as the loyalty and rate of retention of each. Furthermore, the culture will determine how the business operates overall, how it develops new products, manages costs, finds new streams of revenue, and exhibits your advertising and marketing. Even more important, it presents the company's narrative. It is the background against which all of this happens, or, more accurately, it is the spirit, ambience, and atmosphere within which all business transactions occur. That your culture expresses your values means you can't focus on it, then on the business, or vice versa. They are different strata of the same process and must be addressed simultaneously. Pay attention to every subtlety and intricacy of how you do business, and your culture will eventually become apparent.

✓ **Establishing a culture committee:** Enlist a group of people from diverse departments who are dedicated to creating a culture brand that conveys what everyone who works there already feels: It is an organization where people love to work, and with which other companies enjoy doing business. Ask this team to help you identify the consistencies and inconsistencies between the values you espouse, those you practice, and those that the current culture express. The group members' role is to close the gap and create an esprit de corps in sync with the company's history and identity. Leaders need to help them appreciate their less obvious, but vital, task: resuscitating the company's past by uncovering, preserving, and protecting the narratives of the organization's history and the stories of earlier generations of employees.

Make it clear to the rest of the organization that this

committee's mission is a strategic priority. For example, you can have one of the company's top three executives lead the group. At Synovus, CEO Jim Blanchard spends half a day every month with his committee. Colleen Barrett, president and COO of Southwest Airlines, started the culture committee at her company, and continues to be closely involved. Chairman Herb Kelleher, Vice Chairman Jim Parker, and many other Southwest senior executives have joined Barrett by contributing to the committee. Ernst & Young's Alan Kline, American director of tax operations, attends all the culture team's meetings; and GSD&M's Roy Spence, president, leads the culture initiatives at Idea City. Like all leaders, they allocate their time to their own priorities. But what distinguishes Barrett, Kline, Spence, Blanchard, and others is that their priorities' axis, around which all else rotates, is their companies' cultures. Their presence declares more loudly than any verbal exhortation what they value and what's important at their organizations.

✓ Creating a burning platform: There is no question that it is far more difficult to change an existing culture than to initiate a new one. Since little stimulates culture change faster than a crisis, create one if it's not already ongoing.

When teamwork faltered at Southwest Airlines, Herb Kelleher, who felt the culture could be at risk, gave a speech on "tribalism" (or wars within a culture) describing how infighting impoverished and destroyed certain tribes. Then he illustrated the parallels to some of the contentiousness he was sensing inside Southwest. He predicted that the same destructive forces could hurt Southwest employees' job security and livelihood. Understanding that before people will embrace a change in culture they must be sufficiently dissatisfied with the old one, Kelleher focused a persuasive case on the possible alarming effects of infighting or tribalism to use his terms.

Here are some of the possible worrisome repercussions to complacency in not dealing with tribalism within an organization. If you find them relevant to the state of your business or your culture, they can help you build a powerful case for change:

- **Talent.** If we don't change our culture, our best people will leave. Not only will that cost us millions of dollars in attrition, but we will lose the talent we need to remain competitive.

- **Personal.** If we don't change the culture and in turn lose business and revenues, we will be less capable of providing for our families and realizing our dreams.

- **Speed.** If we don't relinquish control over people and begin to trust them, we will not be prepared to respond to market changes with alacrity. If we fail to provide immediate solutions to anticipated customer needs, which in our current culture is likely, then we will begin a downward slide from which recovery will be difficult, if not impossible.

- **Technology.** If our culture remains unwilling to leverage the power of technology, our obsolescence is right around the corner.

- **Competition.** While we spend our time fighting turf battles, pursuing rivalries, nursing jealousies, and holding grudges, our competition is advancing against us, preparing to leave us in the dust.

- **Ethics.** If we don't remember or relearn our values and the importance of emphasizing them, we have no right to be surprised if we find ourselves in the midst of a scandal, like those we've all been reading and talking about.

CHAPTER 3

Gutsy Leaders
Create a Sense
of Ownership

What gives people at some companies the discipline to transcend petty politics and competition to concentrate on building a better organization? The answer is that they feel more like owners than just employees of the business. Owner-employees are inspired to take responsibility because their own success and that of the business are intricately linked. They know they are part of something special, and their pride motivates them to care and act in extraordinary ways.

Gutsy leaders know that giving employees ownership and responsibility is a way of saying, "I trust you, I believe in you, and you are an integral part of this company's success." When you walk into organizations where employees don't have a sense of ownership, you find a psychological wall between those individuals and the company. This atmosphere is precisely what Dilbert represents—the soulless world of corporate cubicles in which people show up, do the minimum, assume no responsibility, avoid the landmines, and collect a paycheck. It's a waste for the individual, who is locked in an unfulfilling cycle of mediocrity, and it's a waste for the organization, which fails to capitalize on the gifts and talents of people who are capable of far more than they are achieving.

Ownership is a powerful force that can inspire even the most productive workforces to surpass themselves. Whole Foods, the nationwide chain of gourmet organic and natural-food stores, operating in an industry notorious for its workers' indifference, is just one of many remarkable enterprises that are unparalleled regarding their empowered, motivated, and entrepreneurial employees. As you read its story, imagine the possibilities if everyone in your company had the same spirit.

Whole Foods—Power to the People

The concepts of teamwork, autonomy, empowerment, and ownership have become shopworn clichés in much of the business world—overused and underpracticed to the point that they have lost all meaning. At Whole Foods, these ideas are the foundation of a business model that is blowing the competition out of the aisles.

Whole Foods Market began life in 1980 in Austin, Texas, and it hasn't stopped growing since. In 2003, the company had 140 stores in 25 states stretching from the Atlantic to the Pacific. Its $2.7 billion in revenues in 2002 made it the world's largest retailer of organic and natural products, and its net profits of $84 million were double the industry average. Meanwhile, with new stores and acquisitions, its employee count rose to 24,100, a 16 percent leap from the previous year.

So while the supermarket industry has been growing by at most 3 percent a year, Whole Foods sales and revenues have been rising by double digits for years, all through the recession. Over the last five years, for example, its revenues have jumped by an average of 16.4 percent. Oh, yes, don't forget the company's stock price, thumbing its nose at the long bear market to end 2002 at $50.19 per share for a market capitalization of $32 billion.

Part of the company's roaring success is owed to timing—its founder, John Mackey, already was in the natural-food business when the public's anxiety over pesticides and preservatives first ignited the demand for organic, natural produce. The wave is nowhere near cresting, and Mackey has ridden it all the way up. At the same time, he's created stores that are so handsomely designed, efficient, and enjoyable to shop in that he has hijacked customers from conventional grocers.

Some hint of where Whole Foods is heading can be gleaned from a conundrum Mackey likes to offer at company meetings: "Americans love to shop. Americans love to eat. But Americans hate to shop for food." He intends to make shopping for food as much fun as shopping for clothes or anything else, and he's well on his way to achieving that goal.

Timing and know-how aside, Whole Foods is successful because its gutsy founder and chief executive has largely given over the operation to his employees. And they have rewarded him with a level of dedication and loyalty virtually unique in the industry.

The genesis of Whole Foods starts in Austin, Texas, in 1978, with John Mackey's opening of Safer Way Natural Foods with a $10,000 loan from his father. After a merger with another shop, Mackey set up the first Whole Foods Market in 1980 in a counterculture neighborhood of Austin, close to the university students and faculty Mackey assumed would be his best customers. He had it right.

At the time, the health-food business was totally fragmented, and gradually, one by one, Mackey began to pick off his competitors. At first, he usually kept to college towns in Texas; then he moved into neighboring states. By 1992, Whole Foods had expanded to California and was selling its first products under the Whole Foods label. It went public the next year, and used the cash to buy some of the small chains of health-food stores that were beginning to crop up around the country.

From food to natural supplements was a small jump, and Mackey made it in 1997 with the $146 million purchase of Amrion. As new Whole Foods stores opened, they had other amenities, including juice bars and prepared-food sections—almost everything you'd find in the most upscale traditional supermarket. Something else Whole Foods stores had, which you don't find in abundance in most supermarkets, is a pleasant, helpful workforce committed to a healthy environment, healthy foods, and serving the customer. That commitment grows out of a covenant between the organization and its employees: We will make you a fully informed partner in the business, and, in return, you will take full responsibility for delivering stellar performance.

You might say that Whole Foods stands for peace, love—and profits. The company's mission statement is called the "Declaration of Interdependence," and it talks about its relationship to the communities it serves, to its people, and to the planet. "Whole Foods are for everyone," it says. "We create store environments that are inviting, fun, unique, informal, comfortable, attractive, nurturing, and educational. . . . Everyone is welcome, regardless of race, gender, sexual orientation, age, beliefs, or personal appearance."

John Mackey is a hiker and outdoorsman who comes to work in boots and jeans, talks unaffectedly about the beauty of capitalism, and generously praises and compliments people as he travels around the stores. His salary, which is nowhere close to what most *Fortune* 500 CEOs make, can be no more than 14 times his average employee's pay, and far less in the occasional bad year. In 2002, when an ill-judged Internet venture depressed profits, he got only $210,000 and no bonus.

Walk into any Whole Foods store, and you will be greeted by people of every race, nationality, and ethnicity. This diversity is the future of our global economy—and it works. What's more, the company sup-

"I don't see any conflict between **wearing our hearts on our sleeves** and running a company that is **serious about profits**."

ports and celebrates family and organic farming; it gives 5 percent of its profits to charity and is involved in good works in every community where it has a store. But if Whole Foods' values may seem soft, don't be fooled. A hard-core, competitive spirit pervades this place.

As Mackey has said: "I don't see any conflict between wearing our hearts on our sleeves and running a company that is serious about profits. In fact, we feel there is a profound synergy between the two. Both are about responsibility. And our employees, in turn, have a responsibility to deliver the highest-quality food and service to our customers."

Disciplined Democracy

In fact, Whole Foods has evolved considerably from its origins as an earnest dispenser of organic apple juice and wholesome, if slightly blemished, produce. These days, the stores are elegant, pricey, speak to the ideal of harmony with nature, and offer such delicacies as cooked Alaskan king crab legs and chocolate-covered espresso beans. Bins and shelving of warm, polished wood display lovingly tended mountains of gorgeous produce, and casual seating areas tempt shoppers to slow down and join the community. "It's almost impossible to shop at one of these markets," the *Boston Globe* recently gushed, "and not be subtly persuaded—by the store's design and mix of products—that your presence there says something about you. Namely, that you are smart and that you care about your family's health. And, by the way, you are a responsible citizen, buying products that are good for Mother Earth and supporting a food store with a mission to improve the world around it."

At Whole Foods, getting people to think and act like owners starts with leaving them alone. In fact, each store operates as a stand-alone business, catering to local tastes, buying from local sources, and responsible for its own profits. The structure within a store is based on an average of 10 autonomous teams—one each for produce, grocery, cheese, prepared foods, and so on. The team structure then extends upward: Each store's team leaders are a team; each region's store leaders are a team; and, at the top of the apple cart, the company's six regional presidents are a team.

"We aren't interested in hierarchy; we just don't feel it's effective in any way," Mackey explained. "We like to think of ourselves as a democracy, a structured and disciplined democracy. Energy and ideas work their way up, rather than the other way around. When it comes to rules, I believe that less is more."

On small teams, peer pressure is a powerful force. People feel loyal to a team and responsible to their teammates in ways they rarely do to a large organization. "We have found that the more freedom and autonomy we give our people, the more we let them know about how the company works, the more committed and responsible they become," Mackey told *Fast Company*.

Whole Foods has been on *Fortune*'s list of the 100 best companies to work for in the United States for six straight years. Though only 30 percent of employees at grocery retailers nationwide are full-time workers, 87 percent of Whole Foods' employees work full-time, making them eligible for full health benefits, a 20-percent discount on merchandise, and a gain-sharing program that distributes departmental savings to employees. Stock options are available to full-time employees. And Mackey recently decreed a custom called "appreciations": At the end of every meeting, the participants tell what they like about each other and thank each other for help. This enables employees to act on and embrace their philosophy that generosity and caring should be acknowledged.

Insanity That Works

Let us introduce you to Ricardo Semler, a Brazilian who redefines "business as usual" by encouraging people to stretch beyond their self-imposed limits. Surrounding himself with great talent and staying out of their way, this corporate rebel is doing what mild-mannered, conforming types say can't be done. His Brazilian company, Semco, has become world famous for real-world business practices that many observers find "insane" until they see that they work.

Ask someone at Semco, "Who's in charge?" and the most likely response will be, "No one." Semler promotes ownership by radically giving up control.

The company was founded in 1952 by Semler's father, Antonio, and specialized in the manufacture of marine pumps. Ricardo took over in 1980 at the age of 21, his head brimming with radical ideas about how businesses should operate. Within a few days, he had dismissed 75 percent of the senior executives and begun putting his ideas into practice.

A man after our own hearts, Semler urges employees to "go with your guts" in their decision making. That has led to a company with a bewildering number of disparate elements. Among other things, Semco makes industrial machinery like mixers for pharmaceutical and candy companies, builds cooling towers, runs office buildings' data centers, provides consulting services on environmental issues, creates software for Internet applications, and manages human-resources activities for major companies.

According to Semler, his various operations have three things in common. They're complex enough to discourage new competitors from jumping in; their quality and price are on the high end; and they occupy a unique niche in their markets.

They have done well for Semler, racking up an annual growth rate of 24 percent over the last decade and 2002 revenues of $160 million, up from $4 million when he took over—all this despite Brazil's rough economy (four currency devaluations, record unemployment, and hyperinflation). An investment of $100,000 in this convention-busting company 20 years ago would have an approximate value of $5 million today.

Communicate everything you can to your associates. The more they know, the more they care. Once they care, there is no stopping them.

—SAM WALTON

Semco has no job titles, no organizational charts, and no headquarters. If you need an office, you go online and reserve space at one of the few satellite offices scattered around São Paulo. Semler said, "If you don't even know where your people are, you can't possibly keep an eye on them. All that's left to judge is performance." What gets judged at your company, visibility or performance?

Many workers, including factory workers, set their own schedules and their own salaries. They can also choose their own form of compensation based on 11 different options. What prevents associates from taking advantage of this freedom? First, all of the company's financial information is public, so everyone knows what everyone else makes. People who pay themselves too much have to work with resentful colleagues. Not long ago, union members argued that their pay increase was too high and would hurt profitability. Second, associates must reapply for their jobs every six months. Pay yourself unfairly, and you could soon be looking for a new job. Finally, employee compensation is tied directly to the company's profits—there is enormous peer pressure to keep budgets in line.

What gets **judged** at your company, **visibility or performance**?

Employees are encouraged to regularly take off half a day in the middle of the week. They lose 10 percent of their salary, but Semler believes that they should use that time for active pursuits when their bodies can handle it. He also feels that it is stupid to force people into retirement at their intellectual peak.

Workers choose their managers and evaluate them twice a year. The results are publicly posted. Meetings are voluntary; if no one shows up, it means that the topic to be discussed must be untimely or unimportant. At every board meeting, two seats are reserved for employees on a first-come, first-served basis.

Semco has no receptionists, secretaries, or personal assistants. All employees, including Semler, greet their own guests, get their own coffee, write and send their own correspondence, and make their own copies.

Semler, who, of course, has no title, has built a reputation for encouraging people to fearlessly ask "why." Why do we have job titles? Why do we need a headquarters? (According to Semler, "It's a source of control, discrimination, and powermongering.") Why shouldn't employees have access to detailed financial information? Semler believes that challenging assumptions, rather than conforming to them, is the key to building an adaptive, creative organization.

The company has a policy of no policies. Instead, Semco offers employees a 21-page "Survival Manual" filled with cartoons and brief declarations designed to help assimilate people into its culture. Here are a few examples:

- **Organization chart**

  "Semco doesn't use a formal organization chart. Only the respect of the led creates a leader. When it is absolutely necessary to sketch the structure of some part of the company, we always do it in pencil, and dispense with it as soon as possible."

- **Clothing and appearance**

  "Neither has any importance at Semco. A person's appearance is not a factor in hiring or promotion. Everyone knows what he or she likes or needs to wear. Feel at ease—wear only your common sense."

- **Participation**

  "Our philosophy is built on participation and involvement. Don't settle down. Give opinions, seek opportunities and advancement, always say what you think. Don't just be one more person in the company."

If all this sounds like a recipe for chaos and anarchy, consider this. Semco's products are so good and its customer service so efficient that 80 percent of its yearly revenues come from repeat customers. Over the last decade, the company's sales increased by 600 percent and profitability by 500 percent. Equally impressive, with a current backlog of more than 2,000 job applications, Semco has had less than 1 percent turnover among its 3,000 employees in the last six years.

At Semco, employees can't help but think and act like owners of the company. When no one's in charge, everyone is responsible—for acting in the team's best interest, for providing the kind of product and service experience customers demand, and for growing the business. And everyone is accountable for the results.

Ownership Is a State of Mind

Leaders like Whole Foods' Mackey and Semco's Semler know that employees must feel a personal stake in the enterprise's success before they can be expected to step up to the plate. We call this concept shared interest. The gutsy leaders we've met work hard to unleash their people's ingenuity, pride, and passion, and it doesn't happen overnight. They experiment with programs, make their share of mistakes, fine-tune systems, and replicate what works. What remains constant is an unyielding commitment to giving everyone in the organization power and responsibility.

When someone is thinking like an owner, he or she will ask: "Since this is my business, how will I sell this product?" Or "Would I request this piece of equipment for my department? Should I ask for another full-time position? How should I treat my employees?"

Owners step out from behind titles and job descriptions to act on behalf of the customer and the company. You never hear them say, "It's not my job." They never throw problems over functional walls ("Let me transfer you to . . .") or make excuses. Owners cater to the organization's mission, vision, and values; non-owners cater to the boss. Owners focus on the business results of their actions, no matter who is watching; non-owners focus on how they're perceived by the chain of command. Owners have the guts to ask the tough questions. They understand the consequences of complacency, and they aren't afraid to challenge the status quo with the mantra "How can we make it better?" Preoccupied with their own security, non-owners gravitate toward the predictable and less disruptive. Owners disregard functional boundaries to consider what's good for the company as a whole. Non-owners engage in tribalism and turf protection. Owners bend, stretch, or even break rules that don't serve the customer. Non-owners live by the letter of the law even if it is flat-out contrary to common sense.

Owners pay attention to details; non-owners fail to notice. Owners treat the company . . . well, as if they own it.

Teaching Ownership

If you want your people to think and act like owners of the business, you have to do more than just offer profit sharing, provide stock options, and share financial information. You must educate them. It means demystifying the language of business, explaining what the numbers mean, teaching how that information can be applied. At Semco, every employee not only receives the company's financial statements but is encouraged to attend classes on how to read and analyze these reports. Employees must understand how economic value is created, how revenues and expenses translate into profit, how they can create financial security for themselves and the organization, and what investors contribute and want in return.

The founder of Quad/Graphics, the late Harry Quadracci, felt education was so important that he often taught his company's "Introduction to Printing" course. He encouraged any new employee who had not graduated from high school to earn an equivalency certificate. The company shows all employees how to make optimal use of their fringe benefits, and, if they request it, it will also help them open checking and savings accounts. The goal is for each employee to develop a sense of responsibility, both to self and to the organization. Quad/Graphics wants people to understand the link between their fates and the company's: If the enterprise thrives, so will they. Gradually, most of them grow into proud, motivated team members who give the company their hands, heads, and hearts.

For example, at Quad/Graphics, each press crew is considered a profit center that signs its own entries in the company's books. The manager of the crew—the "first pressman," who may be as young as 24—is required to keep daily tallies on production levels and downtime. He or she also has a voice in hiring, firing, and employee scheduling, and almost complete authority in the areas of cost containment, quality control, and customer relations. Quadracci believed firmly that the chief executive's role was to lay down sound principles, then walk away and let people do their jobs.

Ownership requires a sweeping perspective, not a narrow focus on a particular product or service line. It demands great execution in the present with an eye simultaneously kept on the future. Employees must be taught to see themselves as the people who make the business grow. But conventional organizations are designed to do the opposite. Focusing employees on one narrow part of the organization, they send the message, "Take care of your functional area. Let senior executives worry about the company as a whole." This attitude is obviously demeaning (since it assumes that only those at the top are capable of strategic thinking), and it instantly shuts down imaginative, creative thinking. It ignores the fact that the company's success will be determined by the leader's ability to draw upon and leverage the brainpower and heart-power of the whole organization. It practically guarantees mediocrity at best, and invites downright failure.

Real Leaders Liberate Talent

Ownership means that people are free to act without the fears that squash initiative. When employees have to cling to safety nets, they are certainly not going to commit themselves to a system in which they have responsibility and accountability. Self-preservation becomes the norm.

Harry Quadracci pushed his people into thinking like owners and assuming the responsibilities that viewpoint engenders. In one characteristic move, he financed an expansion of the trucking fleet by inducing his drivers to find loads for their return trips. Handing them the keys to their trucks, he announced that they were all now owners in the corporation's new division—DuPlainville Transport. How they made the rigs profitable on return trips was up to them. When the drivers asked Quadracci how to do that, he answered, "I don't know anything about driving an 18-wheeler." To their own amazement, the drivers found loads and made their new division work.

Turn Up the Volume on Trust

Ownership is a radical approach because it recognizes that an organization's true experts are the people on the front lines, and trusts them to operate with the organization's best interests in mind. And that trust will bolster employees' self-confidence and encourage them to take on even more responsibility. Herb Kelleher, Southwest's chairman, once observed, "You build self-confidence when you give people the room to take risks and you give them the room to fail. You don't condemn them when they fail, you just say, 'That's an educational experience and we're going on from here. We've just spent a good bit on your education; we hope to see you apply it in the future.'"

We have little patience for managers who ask, "How can we be sure that people will act responsibly with the level of power you're talking about?" We tell them that some people may disappoint them, but we're willing to bet that the majority of their workforce is made of up individuals who, once they have a financial or emotional stake in the business, will take responsibility for themselves and those close to them every day. (If not, they're making poor hiring decisions.) Most are hardworking dual-career couples. They pay their mortgage or rent on time; they lug their kids to and from school, soccer, piano, and a whirlwind of other activities. They attend church, mosque, or temple. Many are involved in a charity; others are room mothers and Cub Scout leaders. Yet some managers question whether these people can be trusted, whether they can handle the responsibility. Such managers are not just out of touch—they're arrogant. They should have the guts to let go!

Stanley Steemer has built a national chain of franchised carpet-cleaning shops on a base of gutsy leadership. Ask Phil Dean, who operates one of the most successful Stanley Steemer franchises in the United States, what can happen when employees are trusted. His response: "I delegate everything. My feeling is that if somebody's on your butt, one of you doesn't need to be there. And I really push that. I put the decision making at the lowest possible level. It costs money, and it takes time to develop people that way, but I have no turnover with my managers."

When the State of California asked the airlines to use ground equipment powered by electricity instead of gasoline, two of Southwest's maintenance mechanics in Phoenix, Arizona, Rick Denny and John Garamman, sprang into action. In their research, they discovered that a new electric tug—equipment that pushes the plane away from the gate—cost $160,000. NASA engineers said they could convert each tug from gas to electric for $90,000, offsetting the price of replacing the equipment. Still not content, Denny and Garamman figured out how to do it themselves for $27,000, a savings of $133,000 per tug. Converting an average of six tugs at seven locations throughout California would save Southwest $5.5 million; if the airline were to implement the conversion at all of its 58 locations across the United States—which it later did—the company would save $45 million. It's safe to assume that Rick Denny and John Garamman have the satisfaction of knowing that they have made a valuable contribution to Southwest and that their contribution meant increased job security.

The cultures of trusting companies embrace the concept of employee commitment and reject the concept of top-down compliance. In a trusting company, employees are invested in their jobs because they want to be, not because they have to be. The challenges we face today require committed people. And the key to developing them lies in the hands of leaders who know how to liberate talent. There is no better example than SAS Institute when it comes to liberating talent and creating a culture of trust. Jeff Chambers, vice president of human resources, describes the SAS culture as follows: "We try to give our people incredible flexibility so they can get their work done while still living a balanced life. And as a result we have gained this unbelievable trust and loyalty. . . ."

While most who tell the SAS story focus on the lavish perks and benefits that SAS employees receive, that's really not the heart of the

"We want you to have **all the information** you need to **be creative,** and to become **more deeply engaged** in the business."

culture. What makes the SAS culture so trusting and so successful is that every single employee benefit is viewed as a long-term business investment. SAS learned that in order to liberate and engage talented people for the long haul, these same individuals need help in dealing with or minimizing life's daily distractions. Think about it: Give your people whatever they need to better balance work and life, and guess what, they do it! And at SAS they do it really, really well.

Keep No Secrets

The more people know about your business, the more they will care. When an organization keeps secrets, people disengage because they feel left out. Morale and productivity suffer because employees bring less of themselves to work. How can we expect people to think for themselves and work to build a strong, profitable enterprise if they have no idea what goes into creating the bottom line? How can we make them responsible if they don't know how their actions affect the business? We are baffled by CEOs and CFOs who will share financial information with golfing buddies, business reporters, and analysts, but clam up when it comes to the employees who have the biggest impact on the organization's success.

You might be thinking, "Yes, but what if the information we share gets out to our competitors?" We've got news for you: Your competitors already know most of that. Internet chat rooms, former employees, suppliers, and customers, not to mention the media, all are powerful sources of intelligence. In fact, if you want to try something gutsy, get your information-technology or marketing people to identify two or three industry chat rooms and find out what people are saying about your products and your business. How much they know might surprise you. Our advice: Spend more time figuring out how to keep your people on the cutting edge of information and worry less about keeping it away from the competition.

Keeping people informed conveys trust and inspires accountability. It treats people as responsible adults who are fully capable of learning how the business works and who are willing to do what is best for the organization. It tells them, "We want you to have all the information you need to be creative, and to become more deeply engaged in the business."

> Secrecy is the enemy of trust and is responsible for much of the distrust that exists between business and society, corporations and customers, managers and employees.
> —KESHAVAN NAIR

Whole Foods is especially passionate about sharing information with everyone in the company. John Mackey calls it a "no-secrets" management philosophy: "In most companies, management controls information and therefore controls people. By sharing information, we stay aligned to the vision of shared fate."

The curious Whole Foods team member has access to nearly as much operating and financial data as top management. In all stores, there is a sheet posted next to the time clock that lists the previous day's sales, broken down by team. Another sheet lists the sales numbers for the same day the year before. Once a week, sales totals for every store in the company are posted. And once a month, stores get a detailed report that analyzes sales, product costs, wages and salaries, and operating profits for every store. Because the data is so sensitive, it isn't posted publicly, but it is freely available to any team member who wants to see it. And store managers routinely review it with their team leaders. Since individual teams make decisions about labor costs, ordering, and pricing—the factors that determine profitability—the reports are indispensable.

Even the Payroll Is Open

There is more. Once a year, Whole Foods conducts a survey that probes employee attitudes (notice, they are not measuring satisfaction). This is a no-holds-barred exercise that measures employees' confidence in team leaders, store leaders, and regional leaders. It asks about fears, frustrations, and whether or not they believe the company is adhering to its values. Brutally honest stuff—the results of which, you guessed it, become public information.

Ready for the capper? Whole Foods, like Semco, even posts everyone's salaries. This policy is undeniably radical. But in a democracy, openness is strength. The policy banishes the destructive whispers and rumors about who makes what. Every store has a book that lists the previous year's salary and bonus for all employees. And the trust-building payoff is substantial. Mackey initiated the policy in 1986. "I kept hearing that people thought I was making so much money," he recalled. "Finally, I just said, 'Here's what I'm making; here's what cofounder Craig Weller is making—heck, here's what everybody's making.'"

Surprisingly, most employees don't spend much time studying the salary book. Once the novelty wears off, and people discover that the cashier in the next aisle makes roughly what they make, they get on with their jobs. Of course, Whole Foods' approach to sharing information is not for the faint at heart. If you're going to create a no-secrets policy, you'd better have the guts to talk straight with people.

Mackey told *Fast Company* magazine that the open-salary policy does spark disagreements—but disagreements have their uses. "I'm challenged on salaries all the time, but almost always by managers. 'How come you're paying this regional president this much, and I'm only making this much?' I answer straight, 'Because she's more valuable. If you accomplish what she does, I'll pay you what I pay her.' It leads to deeper, more honest conversations. It creates a culture that values authenticity. And that's all to the good. That's part of democracy. If you're trying to create a high-trust organization where people are all-for-one and one-for-all, you can't have secrets." When it comes to information, gutsy leaders let it flow.

Making Strategy Clear to Everyone

Ownership requires the faith and confidence of both employers and employees. As a leader, you must feel confident that when the decisive moment comes, those who have assumed ownership will exercise common sense and good judgment, which is far more likely if the company's strategy has been made abundantly clear to everyone. Teaching your strategy should focus on helping people make the right choice among many. One way of ensuring that is to ask your employees to define what trade-offs are worth making in any particular situation. Encourage them to think about what makes the company unique. If they must make a trade-off, finding the right one will be easier if they have a clear understanding of what the company stands for, where it is going, and its reason for being.

Southwest Airlines provides one example of how this can be accomplished. When people suggest that it should offer assigned seating, Colleen Barrett is quick to ask how that would align with Southwest's core strategy. Yes, Southwest could assign seats, but doing so would lengthen its turnaround times, which would jeopardize its on-time performance record. It would also raise fares by $10 or $15, which its customers don't want to pay. Barrett, like other gutsy leaders, never loses an opportunity to make sure that everyone at Southwest understands the company's strategy. She discusses it relentlessly and rarely misses a chance to capitalize on a teachable moment. It's crucial to understand every aspect of the strategy if you are to assume ownership for its implementation.

While Barrett encourages independence, she knows that people need feedback on whether they are exercising good judgment. If strategy gives people autonomy within clearly established boundaries, then the company's purpose, vision, and values define those boundaries. Though some would argue that boundaries limit creativity, anarchy is not our aim. Southwest's purpose certainly differs from, say, Wal-Mart's purpose, and knowing that difference is crucial. Any owner-employee must be able to answer these questions: What business are we in? Why do we exist? What makes us unique? Providing direction doesn't restrain people's energies. In fact, such guidelines give people the freedom to act.

When a Southwest gate agent in Austin, Texas, was approached by a very distressed customer who spoke only Spanish, her willingness to think like an owner may have saved the man's life. The customer was on his way to Houston for a kidney transplant, and he had mistakenly gotten off the airplane in Austin. The gate agent spoke Spanish, too, and she was able to figure out that not arriving in Houston early the next morning meant that he could lose his chance to get the kidney. She knew there were no more commercial flights from Austin to Houston that night, but she remembered that

Mark Robbins, an Austin ramp agent, was a private pilot. In entrepreneurial fashion, she explained the customer's predicament to Mark, who flew the man to Houston that night. And the gate agent went along for the ride, knowing the customer would be more comfortable having someone else with him who spoke his language. No call was made to the CEO or anyone else to ask permission. The two employees simply handled the customer's problem, knowing that the company would support them.

Once people understand the strategy, they become empowered, knowing that their actions in line with that strategy will be highly valued and considered legitimate and productive by those who share the strategy. Great breakthroughs and extraordinary acts of service usually happen out on the radical fringe of a clearly defined boundary. When boundaries are fuzzy, people get nervous. They tend to cautiously gravitate toward the center of the playing field, where things are safe. When this happens innovation goes out the door, inertia sets in, and it's business as usual.

Teach Business Literacy

How many people on the front lines of your organization understand how revenues and costs translate into profits? How many are capable of interpreting a financial statement? How many would know how much it costs to run their part of the business? Our bet is that 80 percent of your profits come from 20 percent of your customers. Do your people know that? If so, does it affect how they deal with the top 20 percent? How can we expect employees to lower costs and find new revenue-generating opportunities if they have never been taught that side of the business?

The airline industry is notorious for its high operating costs and low margins. When the profit squeeze worsened in the mid-1990s,

Southwest Airlines responded by educating its employees about the razor-thin line between profit and loss. Using the previous year's financial information, a pilot pointed out that lesson by calculating the number of passengers per flight that determined the airline's profitability. The answer was five. Just five customers provided each flight's profit.

The story was printed in Southwest's newsletter, *LuvLines,* and distributed to every employee in the company. How does this new information affect employees? Consider a hypothetical case of two gate agents working an oversold flight. One feels victimized and complains that the reservations people have "done it again." This instinct to blame others will inevitably affect the way this agent treats customers. But the other agent points out that, since just five customers make the difference in their profit sharing, every one of them counts. The second agent works to accommodate those who will not get onto this flight. One is thinking like an owner; the other, like a casualty. Which of them would you want working for you?

They'll Save You Money If They Know Where It Can Be Saved

The crews who clean carpets for Stanley Steemer's Phil Dean can not only give you a job's exact cost, they can break it down by labor, gas and oil, truck and equipment repairs, chemicals, and insurance. They can tell you how many "redos" they did last quarter and the cost of all their service calls. They also know how many paying jobs a crew could not do because they were occupied with "redos."

They know all this because Phil Dean created a powerful orientation process designed to make crew members business literate. For Dean, business literacy means the front line will know that if the franchise does 3,200 jobs per month, and chemicals cost $4.78 per job, the company is spending more than $180,000 a year in chemicals alone. With this information, being precise when doling out chemicals takes on new meaning. At $3.90 per job, the dispatchers know that gas and oil for the fleet costs as much as $12,000 during a peak month. Maybe that explains why they are so passionate about clustering each crew's jobs, instead of having them drive back and forth across town. Dean is following the lead of proponents of open-book management when he says he wants each person on his team to understand precisely why his or her job is so valuable to the business.

Gutsy leaders are secure and smart enough to know that money-saving ideas come from business-literate employees who are fully engaged in discovering new and exciting ways to drive costs down. And they are often successful. In one part of the organization, it may be $10,000; in another, it might be $50,000 or $100,000. At the end of the year, hundreds of small savings can have a huge impact.

For example, when flight attendant Rhonda Holley was collecting empty cups from the cabin, she noticed that Southwest's logo was printed on the plastic trash bag, and two things struck her. First, customers knew which airline they were on, and second, the trash bags were thrown away immediately. She wrote Colleen Barrett to ask how much it cost to print logos on the trash bags. The response thanked her for caring about the company, and added, "You've just saved us $300,000 a year. We're not going to be printing logos on the trash bags anymore."

When employees start thinking this way, there's no telling what can happen in your organization. Creating this level of shared interest requires that your people know the facts.

Make Data Fun

The key to creating business literacy is getting people to internalize the important information you give them, and the medium can determine whether or not this occurs. It's all about design! The way information is packaged is so important that companies spend vast amounts of time and energy creating print ads, Web sites, and annual reports that truly communicate. (Again, the language and words used make a difference.) Yet the same organizations often overlook the importance of designing and packaging information for those who matter most—their employees. Before you complain that people don't read your memos, ask yourself, "Do we package information in a compelling fashion that gets people's attention?" If not, distill your message—and then deliver it in a way that is fun, lively, and easy to grasp. GE's Jack Welch told us, "If a manager can't describe a plan or proposal to me in one slide, I send them back to rework it, because it means they don't understand it very well."

When Southwest Airlines was ready to distribute its mission statement, it contracted with Cracker Jack to insert the document as the prize inside the box. Then each employee received a box. People were so surprised and delighted, they talked about it continuously, and, of course, the talk was as much about the company's mission as it was about the Cracker Jack. The mission statement, ingrained in people's hearts and minds, was fun to learn and interesting to discuss.

Written at an eighth-grade level, Southwest Airlines' annual profit-and-loss statement is illustrated with icons and cartoons, and housed inside a tabloid titled *Plane Tails: Sensational Stories About Sensational Employees*, which is designed as a spoof on the *National Enquirer*. Everyone picks it up because its packaging catches the eye and its contents are easily understood. Consider a young aviator who doesn't have an MBA and doesn't know a lot about business. He picks up a tabloid on the coffee table in the pilots' lounge. The pilot reads and understands the company's profit-and-loss statement because of the way it was packaged. This employee is now better equipped to think about the entrepreneurial role he plays in managing some of the line items on that P&L.

For example, when pilots read that the company spent $500 million in jet fuel in a single year, they now understand the magnitude of jet-fuel prices on the corporation's cost structure—and on his or her own bottom line. Armed with this knowledge, they start looking for new ways to reduce their fuel-burn rate in flight and still get customers to their destinations safely and on-time. For example, the pilots can save money by flying at a different vector (a more direct route) or at a different altitude (a plane burns less fuel at higher altitudes). Southwest Airlines flies approximately 3,000 flights a day, 365 days a year. If every pilot engaged in reducing the fuel-burn rate by just $5 or $10 per flight segment, it could save the company as much as $10 million a year. The savings are significant when you consider that fuel accounts for approximately 20 percent of Southwest's expenditures.

Design Matters

So, if you want your employees to read, respond to, engage with, and talk about information, consider presenting it in a playful yet informative way. (See pages 92–93 for an example.)

Insist on Accountability

How's this for gutsy? An auto dealership gives you a 100-percent guarantee that if it doesn't fix your car right the first time, it will fix it again, then refund all your money. We screwed up, so here's your money back! It's audacious, and only one of many things that differentiate Planet Honda from every other dealership out there. Tim Ciasulli insists on his service technicians' accountability because he is passionate about the dealership's accountability to its customers. Through interviews and focus groups, Ciasulli and his team learned that bringing the car back a second time for the same repair is at the top of a customer's list of complaints. As Ciasulli told us, "It's a

SOUTHWEST AIRLINES REVEALS 1996 PROFIT FORMULA

Southwest Airlines is in the business of carrying Customers, as well as Cargo and Mail, from point A to point B. In 1996, Southwest carried 49,621,504 Customers and 226 million pounds of Cargo and Mail. Money collected from this service is known as **OPERATING REVENUE**.

$3.406 billion

From **OPERATING REVENUE,** the following costs must be subtracted. These costs are known as **OPERATING EXPENSES**:

-$1 billion

1. Since our Employees are our most important asset, it's no surprise that's where most of our expenses go—almost one-third as a matter of fact. Salaries and the cost to provide benefits such as healthcare and Profit$haring for our 24,104 Employees are included in **SALARIES, WAGES & BENEFITS.**

2. **FUEL & OIL** represent the cost of jet fuel required to fly the Southwest fleet.

-$485 million

3. The cost to repair and maintain the Southwest fleet is called **MAINTENANCE MATERIALS & REPAIRS.**

-$253 million

4. For every ticket sold through a travel agent, Southwest must pay a ten percent commission. This is included in **AGENCY COMMISSIONS.**

-$141 million

5. Southwest often sells and simultaneouly leases back its aircraft as a way of financing additional aircraft purchases. The rental payments made to the new owner of the planes are included in **AIRCRAFT RENTALS.**

-$191 million

6. **LANDING FEES & OTHER RENTALS** represent our airport costs.

-$187 million

7. **DEPRECIATION** is an allowance for the usage of aircraft. For example, in 1996, Southwest spent $677 million to add 22 aircraft and related assets. Since the aircraft will last for many years, the entire $677 million does not have to be expensed in 1996. Rather, an allowance is taken for the estimated usage of the fleet during the year.

-$183 million

8. All other operating expenses such as our advertising, communications costs, insurance, property taxes, and the 4.3 cent per gallon federal jet fuel taxes are included in **OTHER OPERATING EXPENSES.**

-$615 million

The sum of Items 1–8 is our **TOTAL OPERATING EXPENSES**.

-$3.055 billion

The difference between our **TOTAL OPERATING REVENUE** and **TOTAL OPERATING EXPENSES** is known as our **OPERATING INCOME**.

$351 million

9.  **OTHER EXPENSES** include nonoperating expenses such as our net interest expense. Since our profits are not sufficient to cover the costs of all the airplanes we add each year, we have to borrow money.

-$10 million

The difference between our **OPERATING INCOME** and **OTHER EXPENSES** is our **INCOME BEFORE INCOME TAXES**.

$341 million

10. And finally, we must pay our state and federal taxes.

-$134 million

And what's left is **NET INCOME—OUR PROFITS!**
(This equates to an average of $4.18 per Customer.)

$207 MILLION

So where do **OUR PROFITS** go? **OUR PROFITS** are used to help pay for our aircraft purchases so that we can grow and provide job security and opportunities for our wonderful Employees.

NET PROFIT MARGIN is the percentage of what's left of total revenues. In 1996, our **NET PROFIT MARGIN** was 6.1 percent — 6.1 cents of every $1 of revenue.

As a result of **OUR PROFITS**, Southwest was able to make a very generous $60,000,000 contribution to our **PROFIT$HARING PLAN**. The contribution to our Profit$haring Plan is included in the **SALARIES, WAGES & BENEFITS** deduction. In 1996, this represented an 8.04 percent increase in annual salaries for eligible Employees. In addition, the Company contributed $35 million to our 401(k).

Is this good performance? Yes, it is good, especially compared to many of our competitors. However, our competitors have been known to lose money, cut wages, and furlough their employees. Therefore, simply beating our competitors is not a good goal.

We want to provide job security, ample Profit$haring for our Employees, and job opportunities offered by Company expansion; and the only way to ensure this will happen is to meet our goal of **7.5 PERCENT NET PROFIT MARGIN**—7.5 cents of every $1 of revenue each year. Since we fell short of our goal in 1996, that means we ALL have to work even smarter and harder in 1997!

What can you do to help meet our goals? It's simple—continue to provide that famous Positively Outrageous Service to our valued Customers and reduce costs wherever possible. Southwest Airlines is a SYMBOL OF FREEDOM, and if we want to continue to bring Americans low fares, we must keep our costs down. If EACH one of us strives to be more productive, efficient, and i... costs. And Southwest Airlines will remain a SYMBOL OF FREEDOM f...

Southwest Airlines makes it easy for anyone to understand the bottom line with their creative packaging of a profit-and-loss statement.

Planet Honda's idea of accountability.

complete waste of time, and time is money." Planet Honda repairs 30,000 vehicles a year; these days, fewer than 1 percent of them return because the car wasn't fixed right the first time.

When Ciasulli offered this radical guarantee to customers, he was raising the performance standards for technicians. Planet Honda openly posts weekly "fix it right" charts detailing the record of each mechanic. A technician who doesn't fix a vehicle right the first time doesn't get paid to fix it the second time.

Since that could cost up to $500 in lost pay for a mechanic who messes up overhauling a transmission, you can imagine the resistance from the technicians' union. But Ciasulli convinced the union that he wanted to enhance his technicians' skill levels and pay rate by building an "A" shop. This meant accelerating the usual time it took for a technician to achieve the highest level of certification. While it ordinarily takes a mechanic seven to eight years to move from a "C" to an "A" rating, at Planet Honda, it now takes three. Ciasulli's strategy has made the union happy, because its technicians are moving into higher-paying jobs faster; the dealership has increased productivity and a more flexible service operation; and the customers couldn't be happier, because they have a guarantee they can't get anywhere else.

Ciasulli attributes his success to the fact that he helps people create better lives for themselves. He helps customers by taking the aggravation out of buying and owning a car, and he helps the technicians get to the highest skill level quickly. Ciasulli is quick to point out that none of this would be possible if information were not readily available to everyone. People must know the company's target and have ways of continually measuring their performance against that standard. This feedback gives employees the satisfaction of knowing they are performing well, or the knowledge that they have to do better.

Make It Clear What Everyone Contributes

At Quad/Graphics, no one can hide mistakes, and everyone can measure his or her performance against everyone else's. Furthermore, every year, management shares financials with the entire workforce.

Southwest's "Plane Tails" takes an inventory of each department's major milestones, so you learn, for example, that:

- **The audit department performed 125 audits, resulting in cost recoveries of more than $1 million.**
- **The reservations agents handled 81 million calls, and the ramp and cargo departments moved 6 million pounds of mail throughout the system.**

Southwest Airlines

PLANE TAILS

Sensational Stories About Sensational Employees

1995 in Review

Deja Vu Vu Vu Vu!

An Inside Look At
The Only 4-Time
Triple Crown Winner
Southwest Airlines

The
Stories
From 1995
You Can't Stop
Talking About!

Southwes
Orbit Th
12,372
See Pag

PLUS

Birdr
Discov
Incredible Deta

Getting the word out
tabloid style has
helped Southwest
Airlines make critical
information fun, rele-
vant, and interesting.

- The finance department processed 789,773 invoices for payment.
- The cleaners cleaned 17,760 aircraft.
- The executive office team assisted Jim Parker (CEO and vice chairman), Colleen Barrett (president and chief operating officer), and Herb Kelleher (chairman) with an astonishing 9,094 pieces of mail on top of 40,000 birthday and anniversary cards.

The free flow of information lets people appreciate how hard their colleagues work. Employees feel accountable to one another and begin to take pride in and care more about one another. They recognize that one department's results affect everyone else, and that everyone is in this together. When people naturally reach across the boundaries of departments and job descriptions to help each other, you know you've achieved ownership.

Jettison Class Mentality

Nowhere are our class divisions more apparent than in the corporate arena. They are the antithesis of the meritocracy that every successful enterprise must strive to be. Relying on stereotypes to form opinions of others reflects a lazy intellect that can't be bothered thinking about each person as an individual. When you pigeonhole someone based on your view of his or her job description, salary, or education, you limit that person's ability to contribute to your company. Inevitably, you will stifle that individual's imagination, initiative, sense of responsibility, and, most important, his or her investment in the organization.

Leaders who are serious about leveraging the knowledge of every person in the enterprise must be adamant about confronting these ingrained views. People who are oppressed under a class system psychologically check out and become order takers and robots. This is the antithesis of ownership and accountability. If you want people to become engaged in making the business better, seeing problems and owning them, they've got to feel important. For example, when an airline assumes that an 18-year-old ramp agent loading bags on the tarmac is too young, indifferent, or uneducated to read a financial statement, it is trapped in a class mentality. This view is destructive in three ways. First, it strips the worker of dignity and lowers morale. It's another way of ensuring that power resides at the top, and that the gap of inequality between people remains wide. Second, it steals talent from the organization by not capitalizing on people's knowledge. In the most basic terms, the company pays for insight it never receives, and deprives itself, in this case, of a young person's potential. If you're playing to win, every mind must be fully engaged.

If you're playing to win, every mind must be fully engaged.

Finally, such discrimination crushes entrepreneurial spirit—and not only that of the specific person involved. Since it proves that anyone at all may be the next target, any hope of building shared interest is shattered. The organization will suffer because, as our examples demonstrate, no one in senior management knows or can do everything. Stereotypical assumptions about class kill everything you're working toward, including profits.

Do "Whatever It Takes"

Does presenting a profit-and-loss statement at an eighth-grade level with pictures and icons seem condescending? Think again. If a financial statement is written in accountant-speak, no one, perhaps including you, will look forward to reading it. Do you look forward to reading your P&L? Why would front-line workers force themselves to plow through such a report, and then discuss what little of it they did comprehend? In these circumstances, most people would prefer that you tell them what to do, rather than engage them in a conversation in which they will feel stupid. You can't build shared interest without a shared language.

Another problem occurs when employees' lack of knowledge is misconstrued as apathy. Of course, people care, but the information they receive—such as monthly financial reports—is impenetrable. And, of course, no one confronts management about that, because doing so would be admitting incompetence.

Though many companies include "dignity and respect" within their values, they don't employ those values when they're really needed, such as when it's time to disseminate information. You need to assess whether your information is either too complicated or too mundane to capture your people's interest.

Southwest firmly believes that individuals must take responsibility for their own learning, but, at the same time, the company recognizes its obligation to do "whatever it takes to get people connected, whatever it takes to help them understand." Gutsy leaders value their front-line employees' intelligence, creativity, insight, and capacity to make significant contributions. And they know that an emphasis on class will annihilate everything they are trying to build.

Make It Personal

In the aftermath of the dot-com explosion, we came across a high-tech company that obsessed about its stock price as a measure of investor confidence. From the outside looking in—and based on what employees told us—the whole focus was on pressuring people to "blow out" the numbers at the end of each quarter. Every time senior management had a difficult call with analysts or major shareholders, employees would get their emotional chains jerked. It wasn't surprising that turnover was high and morale was low. What the company's leaders seemed to have overlooked is that most people come to work for personal reasons, as opposed to pleasing shareholders or making outrageous amounts of money for owners. Organizations with high morale, not high turnover, strive to create a healthy environment that enables its employees to achieve their dreams.

Of course, we understand the need to pay attention to the numbers. But, if that's all that you talk with employees about, they feel taken advantage of. In contrast, when people are hired at Planet Honda, Tim Ciasulli talks to them about how the dealership can help them accomplish their dreams and goals in life. He wants to know the individual behind the salesperson or technician, and he wants Planet Honda to be a vehicle through which they can realize their vision. In fact, every week Ciasulli and the leaders who report to him discuss their highest priorities for that week, both personal and professional. He expects these leaders to do the same with their teams.

When Herb Kelleher talks to the people of Southwest Airlines about a competitor, he rarely emphasizes shareholder value. His interest is always what success or failure means to them personally. He explains the consequences of losing a fare war in the context of its relevancy to their personal lives.

At Southwest, ramp agents, flight attendants, and pilots all know that, on average, a takeoff delay of just 30 seconds can mean less in profit sharing, increased wage concessions, and lowered job security, all of which would have tremendous impact on their lives. It would also mean less money for the catastrophic fund, which helps employees in crisis. The company's contributions to charities, such as the Ronald McDonald houses nationwide, could also be jeopardized. Employees have learned that they are responsible for protecting what matters most to them, and they do. For example, Colleen Barrett tells the story of a new pilot who saw a flight attendant cleaning up the gate area in between flights and reminded her that doing so wasn't in her job description. The flight attendant fired back, "I know, but it is part of my profit sharing." It isn't unusual to see Southwest pilots loading bags when it's 90 degrees on the tarmac in order to get a delayed flight back on time. In fact, Captain Moose Millard told us that the pilots have an unwritten rule: After completing their cockpit check, they look for the busiest person around and pitch in. Again, everyone from the pilots, to the flight attendants, to the chairman must have a whatever-it-takes mentality.

Do you feel this way about your employees? Have they made the explicit connection between the success of the company and their own success? Establish a way of frequently reminding employees of the relationship between their job performance and business results. Then show them how those business results affect their lives. Have the guts to be interested in your employees' personal lives.

Celebrate Your Heroes

Your people's excitement and enthusiasm are the most important resources you have. Unfortunately, they are also the most perishable. With this in mind, Southwest's leaders devote their own time and energy to nourishing the entrepreneurial spirit. Primarily, they do this by recognizing heroes and telling their stories in the company

Establish a way of frequently **reminding employees** of the **relationship** between their **job performance** and **business results.** Then show them how those business results **affect their lives**.

newsletter, or starring them in videos that are distributed company-wide. For instance: the mechanic who changed a tire on a landing gear in six minutes so that a plane could fly on time; the provisioner who spent his own time designing an ice chest for the trucks that will decrease melting and reduce the amount of ice a station needs by 45 percent; the flight attendant who brought a distressed, elderly passenger home with her for the evening, then made sure she was on another flight the next day; the skycap who parked a late customer's car so the customer could make his flight.

These are examples of sensational service and what it means to act like an owner of the company. Their implicit message is "This is the standard we're trying to uphold." And often they inspire people to become heroes in their own jobs, from which a culture of owner-ship emerges.

Sometimes Southwest's recognition comes in the form of a spon-taneous celebration. When Southwest Captain Roger Ways discovered in midflight that his landing gear would not extend, he managed an emergency landing without incident. How? While he was still in the air, he'd gotten input from as many experts as he could. Customers later said the captain had "fluttered" the plane in, and it was one of the smoothest landings they'd ever seen. When she heard that he had arrived at headquarters, Colleen Barrett interrupted a board meeting, emptied the corporate offices, and directed everyone to the atrium. Then she and Herb Kelleher escorted Captain Ways to a balcony so that the 500 people below could give him a resounding ovation. Naturally, the pilot appreciated this support. But just as important, everyone in the company saw and heard it loud and clear.

It was no accident that Captain Ways later wrote to every passenger on the flight to express his appreciation for their cooperation. As we pointed out earlier, how your people treat your customers reflects the way their company treats them.

What do you do when people act heroically in your organization? Do you publicize it? Given the right culture, getting people to act extraordinarily is not the challenge; what you have to do is make sure that these stories are shared immediately. You have to understand the value of acting instantly and spontaneously, as Colleen Barrett did when Captain Ways unexpectedly turned up. It works so well at Southwest because people can rely on the fact that if they send a story to employee communications or the executive offices, it will be broadcast far and wide the next day.

Reward Intelligent Failure

Tim Ciasulli is also a big believer in celebrating successes—and even, on occasion, failures. "At Planet Honda, we celebrate people for taking a chance, even if the outcome isn't the greatest," he said.

"We had a woman who brought her car in for service and was adamant that she needed it back the next day. She said don't touch it unless you can get it back to me on time. Well, the mechanic thought that he could, but when he got started he realized that the problem was bigger than he thought and would take two days to fix. So when she came in, he loaned her a demo car. She goes out and has a fender bender. No one was hurt, but the car was pretty banged up. The accident wasn't her fault, but she felt terrible. She didn't want him to lose his job. There was no chance of that. He got a promotion, and everyone in the company knew why."

Give People a Stake

Gutsy leaders believe that when people become fully engaged in the business, they should participate in the financial success they helped create. When this happens, a very powerful emotional bond between the organization and the employee is formed.

The people of Southwest Airlines care about their company. Employees own 13 percent of it. It is no surprise that when people have an emotional, intellectual, and financial investment in the business, they are more cost-conscious, industrious, and imaginative. Since 1990, Southwest has contributed an average of $180 million a year to profit sharing, which is based on average net profits of $625 million a year. This means that, on average, 13 percent of the employees' annual income came from profit sharing. Over the years, many people at Southwest have become financially independent based on their stock ownership.

TD Industries, a Dallas, Texas, based mechanical and electrical contractor, is another organization in which everyone has a piece of the rock. In 2002, the privately owned company had sales of $217 million, an increase of almost 6 percent over the previous year. The company's 1,400 employees install plumbing, air-conditioning, and ventilation equipment in commercial and industrial buildings.

In 1948, the TDI founder, Jack Lowe, began to distribute non-voting shares to his employees. So, in the 1980s, when the corporation was devastated by an oil-price collapse, it was a natural step for Jack Lowe Jr., who succeeded his father as chief executive, to turn to the employees for help. Led by the Oak Room Council, a group of 150 workers with a minimum of five years of service, the employees voted to return $1 million from their overfunded pension plan. Then, in what Lowe describes as an act of extraordinary courage, the employees contributed an additional $1.25 million from their 401(k) retirement funds in exchange for company stock. This time, the stock came with voting rights. Because they understood that their interests and the company's were one and the same, they now own a nice chunk of the enterprise.

Whereas profit sharing and stock options can be powerful incentives for getting people to think and act like owners, we believe they must be offered in the context of an appropriate environment that supports and educates people on how best to use these motivational tools. As we have said, people think and act like owners because they are equipped, encouraged, and expected to do so. In this context, adding profit sharing and stock options rewards and reinforces people for behaving in ways that are consistent with an already established culture. Thus, you leverage the power of the incentive.

Okay, it's resolved: Getting people to think and act like owners of the business is a powerful competitive advantage, but is it enough for a gutsy leader to blow the competition off the field? No. Building an organization that people are willing to fight for also requires leaders who genuinely love their employees and their customers.

✓ **Change the people who make the rules:** Ownership doesn't only mean changing the rules; it means changing the people who make the rules. Suppose you were to allocate the freedom to hire employees, set targets, and establish schedules to those in your company closest to the front lines. Chances are, those employees would feel more committed and work more productively because they would know that their opinions are trusted and that they are considered the experts of their world.

Examine the significant areas in your organization and find five where you can relinquish control and trust your people to do the right thing. If anyone habitually abuses this freedom, deal reasonably but firmly with him or her.

✓ **Make everyone accountable:** Embrace this mantra: If you're aware of a problem, it's yours. That concept should be embedded in your culture, and be an integral element of how work is done. We don't mean that those who identify the problem are necessarily responsible for solving it, but they are obligated to marshal the appropriate resources to ensure that it is addressed. Establish an ironclad rule that under no circumstances does anyone ignore or walk away from a problem, regardless of whose area it falls in.

✓ **Reward intelligent failure:** People often hesitate to assume responsibility for their honest failures until they are assured that it is safe to do so. Despite your entreaties to initiate projects, take risks, speak their minds, and confront the boss, employees still fear that doing so could jeopardize their jobs. In this area, one thing is certain: People will not overcome that fear until they witness someone rewarded publicly for an intelligent failure. When you explain to your employees that failure is often the forerunner to success, they must trust that you will treat them accordingly.

✓ Quiz your front-line people to see how business literate they are: How many people on the front lines of your organization understand how the company makes money? How many know how to read a financial statement? Who knows how much it costs to run their area of the corporation?

If your business is a car dealership, do your employees know the volume each service bay must yield to earn a profit? Could they tell you the number of new and preowned cars that determined last quarter's profits? If the business is financial services, do they know how many loans you need to make before you cross the break-even point and move into net interest margin? If you find errors in 5 percent of the loan documentation orders, are people familiar enough with the figures to know the cost of correcting them? How about the amount lost when someone in the call center has to make three calls instead of one to resolve a dispute? How many times did something comparable happen last year? If you manufacture heavy equipment, who can tell you the cost of a service technician's extra hour drive to retrieve a part that is needed only because engineering didn't originally use a standard size?

People at all levels of your organization will start to ask questions like these, but only if you teach them to think about the business this way. Help your associates psychologically make the transition from having a worker-identity to an owner-identity by inviting them to point out unnecessary waste and redundancies; then, whether you take their advice or not, reward them, in public if possible, for doing so.

✓ Launch a business-literacy campaign: Understanding how revenues and costs translate into profits is what makes people business literate. Here are some ways of initiating it:

Following the lead of Semco, Stanley Steemer, and Southwest Airlines, simplify your financial statements, then teach your employees to read and analyze them.

If you don't already know it, figure out your break-even point, then communicate it clearly and vividly. Illustrate the ripple effect of $1 of sales. For example, ask them to consider how might Sears's salespeople be affected if they knew that 3 cents of every dollar represents profit? Would they watch costs and serve customers more conscientiously? Would Sears feel the difference?

Keep your presentation simple. Remember that you're not trying to teach the intricacies of accounting. Instead, find relevant measurements, such as: What is the profit earned per product?

In fact, you can turn your teaching into a game. Delta Airlines' business-literacy campaign, called "Our Airline, Our Business," has a board game based on running an airline as the centerpiece of its all-day event. A roll of the dice determines revenues and expenses, and chips represent costs, such as labor and fuel. Interdepartmental teams fill out balance sheets and income statements, expand or contract routes, allot shareholder dividends, and assume debt. As a result, workers realize—and more important, care about—the financial ramifications of nearly every aspect of the operation, from lost luggage, to discounted tickets, to bad weather. Learning about revenues, the hiring process, and food services, just to name a few of the factors that constitute running a sprawling company in a brutally competitive industry, they become better employees in every way.

About this process, aircraft mechanic Paul Blair said: "Before I took the class and played the game, I didn't understand . . . the numbers that we hear back on the floor. Now the cost-savings measures make more sense. . . . In a lot of ways, a big business is just like your home budget. . . . [Since] I didn't really understand how Delta, with all the millions in revenues, could lose money, I resented being asked to give back. Now I see that it really is necessary."

✓ Pay attention to design and how you package information: How your information is designed determines whether or not you are conveying it in an exciting, eye-catching fashion. Is your layout unusual and COMICAL, or is it the same as every other company's? Is the message relevant and inviting, or do people have to grit their teeth to read it?

Indeed, if you want people to look forward to receiving the information, seek their feedback on how you package it now and how you might present it more attractively. We suggest that you get input from individuals and focus groups before running a print ad or commercial spot. It won't surprise you to know that people internalize and are influenced by information that is designed and packaged well—and vice versa.

Here are some ways to create an impression. Display your financial statements graphically with cartoons and icons. Tailor the level of your presentation to one that everyone will understand. Deliver critical information so that it entertains, which will make it easy to remember and the subject of conversation. You might embed it within a puzzle, or, as Southwest did, in a Cracker Jack box.

✓ **Tell a story:** That stories make the theoretical real is a teaching technique that educators have employed for decades. Take advantage of it. By dramatizing information, stories make flat, boring information speak to and inspire us. Create vivid narratives about how small, daily savings add up to huge numbers at the end of the year. We all love stories, and if you narrate them well, people will remember the point or lesson you're conveying. The strategy, however, has one important caveat: You have to be a good storyteller, otherwise you'll bore people and the technique will backfire. But don't despair—you don't have to be born with this gift to excel at it. All you have to do is apply the same effort that you would to any other skill you choose to master. Tell the story over and over and pay attention to people's reactions. Adjust the way you tell the story based on what you learn.

CHAPTER 4

Gutsy Leaders
Hire People
Who Don't Suck

There are people who can find opportunity in any adversity. Good-humored and optimistic, they make life fun. They inspire enthusiasm and are willing to try new things. And we're all better for having them around.

Then there are people who can find the difficulty in every opportunity. They are cynical, sarcastic, and pessimistic. They hate what they do and complain about everything. They sap our energy, and we gain nothing from their presence.

Which kind of person do you want to hire? We

Know Your Target

think the answer is obvious. Moose Millard, a dear friend of ours, once said, "Bad attitudes suck! They suck the passion, energy, teamwork, unity, and life right out of your organization." That's why the strategic hiring philosophy of nearly every gutsy leader we know is to hire people who don't suck.

The Hiring Conundrum

The biggest challenge is not building a company of bricks and mortar, but establishing one of hope, love, service, freedom, communication, fun, and trust. These values create, protect, and promote your corporate reputation, your culture, and, ultimately, your ability to attract and keep the right people. GSD&M, Planet Honda, SAS, Synovus, and USAA are organizations that understand the importance of these values. Clearly, it isn't easy to discover or rediscover your corporate values and core purpose, but it is necessary, since they are the basis for your hiring decisions. Your corporate community will not accept a new employee who is not compatible in these areas. He or she will sabotage your organization's future.

Keep in mind: Now is not the time to be hiring with a shortsighted perspective. The U.S. Bureau of Labor Statistics is predicting that by 2010 only 157 million workers in the United States will be available to fill 167 million jobs. If you think finding the right talent is tough now, just wait a few years.

Finding the Right Fit

Finding highly talented people is only the first step. They have to be ready and able to do what you need doing, and they have to be the right fit for your organization.

Have you defined what it takes to be a great employee in your company? Identify people who already work for you who fit that description. Then ask their customers, employees, peers, and managers what makes them so effective and easy to do business with.

Take the answers and make a list of the relevant attributes, such as: establishes great rapport with customers; works efficiently; knows the technology better than anyone; has a special knack for helping staff develop; can find humor in difficult situations. From this list, create a profile of a great employee and see to it that new hires match it.

Have you **defined what it takes** to be a **great employee** in your company?

Remember that hiring is a two-way street. The person you want also has to want to be a part of your organization. When you spot your next potential superstar, ask yourself, "Will someone of this caliber find our culture attractive?" If the answer is no, figure out why. Is he or she just a mismatch for you, or do you need to work toward changing your culture? If the latter, perhaps this hire would be a first step.

Recruiting Ads That Entice

When you know what you're looking for, find ways of appealing to precisely that kind of person. The next time you've got an open position, ask yourself, "Do our recruiting ads clearly reflect the characteristics and attitudes we want?"

Southwest Airlines, for instance, isn't looking for conventional thinkers with lots of previous airline experience. It wants innovative

SICK OF YOUR JOB?

If you'd prefer a career that's fun and challenging, join the crew reported in *Fortune* magazine as one of "America's Most Admired Companies"—Southwest Airlines. Visit us at www.southwest.com for more information.

SOUTHWEST AIRLINES
A SYMBOL OF FREEDOM

Equal Opportunity Employer

© 1999 Southwest Airlines Co.

> Southwest's unconventional attempt at attracting people despite a tight labor pool.

individuals who challenge conventional wisdom and think outside of the box. Because Southwest has such a clear hiring profile, it is able to design recruiting ads that attract the right people. In areas where unemployment is low, Southwest taps a new kind of labor pool. It printed the question "Sick of Your Job?" on the motion-sickness bags. The company knows that there are individuals who are unhappy or bored with their current jobs and might fit well at Southwest.

Though not every senior executive will do this, Herb Kelleher dressed up as Elvis to pose for an advertisement. The headline read,

The late Harry Quadracci wasn't shy about posing for an ad.

"Work in a place where Elvis has been spotted." The fine print that followed read, "But if you see him dressed as Ethel Merman, just ignore him. We're trying to cure him of that."

Unconventional ads cause you to stop, think, smile, and, most important, attract people with the right attitudes to your company. The subtext is clear for Herb's ad: If you are a fun-loving, irreverent person who likes to work hard and express your individuality, this is the place for you.

National Tax Compliance
MAGICAL TECHNOLOGY
TOUR 2002

Even Alan Kline at Ernst & Young's National Tax Compliance Group had the guts to dress up like a more modern-day Elvis. He dressed as John Travolta of *Saturday Night Fever* for some on-the-job fun.

GET DOWN!   GET FUNKY!
GET TECHNO!

Tailor your entire recruiting campaign, not just your advertising, to the attitudes and attributes you want. Are your ads enticing, and are you tailoring your recruiting ads to the attitudes and attributes you want? If enthusiasm is part of your profile, skip the gray suits and opt for something more sassy and irreverent. One Southwest ad features a flight attendant carrying a drink tray and dressed in khaki shorts and tennis shoes. The caption reads, "Work at a place where wearing pants is optional." If your aim is to hire smart, technical people who are also irreverent, create an ad that says so. When Southwest advertised for people in its systems area, the company created an ad with a picture of a computer disk. The label on the disk read: "Southwest's Systems Department is looking for people who have a lot of internal drive."

Examine your current recruiting ads. What kinds of messages are they sending? Do they distinguish you from other businesses? If so, how? The content of your ads as well as the channels through which you communicate your message tell prospective candidates about your culture and the kind of attitude you expect.

Become World Famous for Hiring

Let's face it, a company is who it employs. Is your company famous for going after great people? Are your hiring practices well known? From their creative recruiting ads and annual reports to their speeches and interviews, gutsy leaders broadcast the message loud and clear: Getting, developing, and keeping the right people are essential to future success; therefore, hiring is a strategic priority.

Remember, you're not only hiring technicians, engineers, software developers, and sales representatives. You're hiring ambassadors, without whom you can't deliver world-class service. And there's one more, not-so-incidental point: You have to live with them. The people you hire today will set the tone of the corporate culture you enjoy— or endure—tomorrow. Kevin once asked the entertainer Garth Brooks if he was scrupulous about hiring only world-class musicians for his band. Garth answered, "After 160 shows, a guy ought to be able to play an E-minor. The question is: What's he like to live with and travel with the other 22 hours a day?"

What gutsy leaders know is that your competitors can copy your products, improve on your processes, undercut your prices, perhaps even match your quality. What they can't replicate are the attitudes of your people.

The High Cost of Lemons

Let's say that the average cost of recruiting, hiring, and training each new person is $20,000. That means if you employ 200 people and have a 15-percent turnover rate, you're hiring 30 new people a year—a cost of $600,000. If you employ 5,000 people, the annual cost is $15 million. And those numbers don't include indirect costs of forming and re-forming teams, falling behind on scheduled work, missing deadlines, higher unit costs, lower margins, lost sales, and upset customers. The solution: Lower your turnover. Hire better people in the first place and give them compelling reasons to stick around. All gutsy leaders take hiring extremely seriously.

Ask yourself: Do you judge job candidates as rigorously as you evaluate . . .

- The needs of a new customer?
- The location of a new facility?
- New industry regulations?

If any of these answers is no, it's time to reevaluate your entire hiring process.

Make Hiring a Strategic Initiative

In many organizations, hiring is a human-resource responsibility, carried out with what we call a "ready-fire-aim" approach. Ready: You have open positions. Fire: You hire people with the right skills and experience. Aim: When they're in, you try to "fit" them into the culture with orientation and training. Good luck!

> Hiring the right people needs to be a corporate strategy, and should, of course, use a "ready-aim-fire" approach. • Ready: Position open. • Aim: Conduct a thorough analysis of the requisite skills, and, equally important, consider the attitudes most compatible with the culture, team, community, and position. • Fire: Once you know what skills and qualities it takes to "fit," the challenge is to establish a rigorous recruiting and screening process designed to ensure you get the right people.
>
> The "ready-aim-fire" approach is certainly more strategic and more effective.

Jeff Chambers, vice president of human resources for SAS, said, "It amazes me how much time our managers spend on hiring. They're not just looking for a specific attitude. They're looking for . . . whether [the candidates] fit within the SAS community. . . . Those who live and work within our culture know in their gut who does and who doesn't fit."

Jill Corsi is executive director of strategic staffing at USAA, the financial-services giant based in San Antonio, Texas. Most of its 5 million customers are military personnel and their families; in 2002, the company provided them with $9.2 billion worth of insurance, banking, brokerage, catalog, and travel services. Jill told us that her company obviously looks for technical skill, but beyond that, it wants outstanding people whom you naturally just want to be around. Since 60 percent of its employees are service representatives, most candidates must perform a call-center simulation and are interviewed according to a customer-service "fit" instrument. Candidates also watch a video that illustrates a day at work in the life of a member-service representative. According to Jill, the video has "helped us weed out people who have an unrealistic perspective of the position. And, on the upside, we get people who say, 'Gosh, this

WE'RE WITH YOU

is a tough job, but I want to do it.' And it gets them even more committed to our mission."

USAA's strategic approach to hiring requires that candidates understand the company and its culture. Its due diligence separates those who "get it" from those who don't. Since USAA is, without a doubt, passionately committed to and proud of its mission, values, and principles, it wants people who know what it means to serve. Corsi said, "We know a culture fit when we see it. People . . . come in and tell us all about the company. . . . They did their research, and they're really excited about what we do. . . . We find that people who come in and just need a job, typically, aren't the ones that are going to make it. We'll always hold out for the ones that really get it!"

When GSD&M moved hiring to a strategic level, the agency's president, Roy Spence, became very involved. Spence told us, "We're on a mission to travel the country looking for the best and the brightest. My job, between now and when I die, is to disrupt the marketplace and find talented people who are nice and convince them to come to work for GSD&M." When asked to tell us what kind of people GSD&M is looking for, Spence said, "The first thing we're looking for is work ethic. If you have an awesome work ethic, then no matter how good or bad you are at what you do, we're going to find a place for you, because you've paid the price by working hard. Unfortunately, these days everybody says, 'Oh, we're not interested in working hard, we want to work smart.' . . . That is absolutely bullshit. Working hard is the prerequisite of working smart."

GSD&M's second critical issue is support for its core values: freedom and responsibility, community, curiosity, restlessness, winning, and integrity. In fact, hiring became a strategic initiative when the company publicized its corporate values, which are etched in concrete within Idea City's rotunda. Spence told us, "At that point, we made sure our people became a strategic strike force."

Spence believes that when a workforce becomes a strike force, magical things can happen. First, your people become the protective guardians of the company's values. Second, the community will not tolerate people who don't understand or embrace those values. Spence believes that values became GSD&M'S most powerful way to go to market and attract great talent.

Finally, GSD&M looks for people who want to make a difference and be a part of a worthwhile endeavor.

"Working hard is the prerequisite of working smart."

Hire Purpose-Driven People

At USAA, GSD&M, Synovus, Fredric's Corp., and so many other companies, leaders and associates alike believe that their work serves a larger purpose than the bottom line alone—and that conviction is built into their hiring practices. What it means to be a company with a purpose is discussed in depth in Chapter 6, "Gutsy Leaders Make Business Heroic." Here, we're interested in helping you incorporate this goal into your process of interviewing and screening potential hires.

"Our purpose is very clear," Spence told us. "We want to represent and help build sustainable results for brands of purpose. . . . If a brand does not have a purpose, we don't want to represent them. If you're not a brand of purpose, then you look to us to solve the purpose, and we can't. We can only bring it to life. We can't create it, but we can help discover it and bring it to life, and that's what we're gifted at. In fact, our branding process has moved from value-based branding to the final frontier of purpose-based branding. So, if you're gonna be the best in the world at representing brands of purpose, you'd better hire people who are purpose driven."

Spence's epiphany—that a culture of purpose must be sustained by people with purpose—effected a powerful shift in screening. In addition to searching for individuals with a good work ethic who support the GSD&M values, recruiters ask each potential hire to explain his or her purpose in life. Spence told of an interview for an important strategy position in which the candidate "confidently, not arrogantly . . . looked me straight in the eye and said, 'I could have been in any business in the world. I just lucked into [advertising], but no matter what [the] business . . . I would have gone in to make a difference.'" Spence was impressed.

Are you hiring people who are interested in any job? Or are you strategically hiring people who love their work and share your purpose? Think about it: Here's a guy who wants to be in a place where what he does matters and makes a difference. People who under-stand, connect with, and commit to and agree with your purpose are more likely to want to contribute their talents to your organization for reasons beyond just doing a job.

According to Spence, "Purpose is powerful stuff! He didn't come here to just make money or just get a job. He came here to make a difference."

Spence, himself, is a leader of purpose. He wants to make a differ-ence. When you talk to him about his work, he gushes with passion and conviction.

"I've never had a job," he confessed, "but I've really worked hard for 31 years, and I love work-ing. I love working in the garden, I love working with my hands. I love working with our clients. I love working for this company. And I love work-ing with all the purpose-driven companies we believe in. I love the concept of work. I'm look-ing at my rose garden right now—70 roses I planted myself at the employee entrance to Idea City. Our people walk by these roses every morning not even knowing I did it, but I know that somehow I put a little bit of happiness and joy in their lives just by my work."

> Keep away from people who try to belittle your ambitions. Small people always do that, but the really great make you feel that you too can become great.
>
> —MARK TWAIN

When he's screening job candidates for Planet Honda, Tim Ciasulli likes to quote Martin Luther King Jr., who said, "A life with-out purpose is a life not worth living." Then he, like Spence, asks candidates: "What's your purpose in life?" Ciasulli believes that candi-dates who are dedicated to improving themselves will be more com-mitted to improving the dealership. He asks, "What do you want to accomplish in the next 24 months? Spiritually, where do you want to be in three years?" One candidate said that he wanted to pay down his mortgage by $65,000. Another said he wanted to lose 35 pounds. Then comes the follow-up question: "Tell me about the plans you have in place to achieve this goal?" The responses reveal a lot about the candidate's vision, values, and ability to plan and execute, all of which are critical to Planet Honda's high-performance culture.

Jill Corsi of USAA told us: "I get teary-eyed every time I share USAA's mission, 'to serve the military . . . individuals who put themselves in harm's way every day to give us freedom,' and, in most cases, the candidates do as well." According to Jill, it's people who identify with and want to serve that higher purpose who are a true "fit" for USAA.

What we've discovered in talking with gutsy leaders is that if you are not driven by a purpose, personally and professionally, you're more likely to become bored with what you do, even if you have made it to the top professionally. Without purpose, the top will feel empty, hollow. In short, when you're hiring, look for people who emotionally connect to a higher purpose. Look for people who want to make a difference and improve their corner of the world; they are more likely to be passionate and enthusiastic. Those who lack purpose will deprive the entire culture of its natural energy.

The Cast Determines the Quality of the Show

When you define yourself as an entertainer whose show intends to make buying a car fun, your dealership becomes your stage. Planet Honda's Ciasulli, who understands that performance is everything when it comes to selling cars, has created an experience that blows customers away. But it works only when he has the right actors, which explains why Planet Honda is so careful about who joins the cast. When your whole brand is based on taking the aggravation out of buying and owning a car, and when your business model is based on "winning customers for life," nothing is more vital to your strategy than attitude.

Ciasulli said, "We look for people with a high IQ and a higher 'I can' outlook." For him, industry experience is of little consequence.

At Planet Honda, performance is everything.

He is much more interested in people who are committed to their own growth in every sense. Job candidates with big ideas and even bigger dreams, who will take risks to make them realities, will fit in at Planet Honda. This company's notion of a big idea is to invite customers into a $150,000 simulator before they take possession of their new cars (more on this later).

One reason that Ciasulli hires for attitude is his unusual expectation that his people approach customers in the role of professional advisers instead of as "salespeople." Salespeople tend to sell what's available on the lot, whereas advisers help the customer determine what's in his or her best interest, regardless of the inventory. Obviously, the difference lies in attitude. The person who cares about the customer's needs asks a lot of questions and truly listens to the answers. Questions such as Where do you normally drive?, How big is your family?, Do you have pets?, and Where do you park? make it clear that the adviser is considering the best solution for this individual or family. Planet Honda people are famous for asking: "What is the best day you've ever had in an automobile?" The mother who describes a serious accident in which she and her two kids walked away unharmed is intensely concerned about safety. The guy who recalls driving along the beach with the top down on his convertible has a very different set of needs. Ciasulli pointed out that his strategy requires altruistic, "other"-oriented people who enjoy this level of closeness with customers. Planet Honda doesn't only sell cars, it helps customers create the ideal driving experiences they envision.

Fired for Attitude

When Tim Ciasulli took over the family dealership, the customer-service ratings were notably low. Investigating the problem, he traced its source to three salesmen. According to him, all three embodied the negative stereotype of the car salesperson. They misrepresented the product, said whatever was required to close a deal, and badgered customers who chose not to buy. Yet they were responsible for selling up to 120 cars per month. They were, by far, the dealership's most productive salespeople. After several attempts to coach and counsel them into using a better long-term strategy failed, Ciasulli had the guts to terminate them. Within a few years, customer-service ratings improved dramatically—and so did sales volume, bringing Planet Honda's national standing to number six. People define success in different ways. For Ciasulli, success isn't the number of cars sold; it's developing relationships with and helping customers. Honoring his commitment to "winning customers for life" gave him the courage to fire three of his best producers.

Would Your Company Hire You Today?

In our opinion, marriage is less about "finding" the right person and more about your "being" the right person. Marriage is a long-term commitment and requires more than a feeling of infatuation for it to work. By the same token, hiring should be looked at as a long-term commitment that requires more than a temporary or convenient set of skills.

Now, if you buy into our thought that marriage is about being the right person, then perhaps you'll buy into the thought that hiring is about being the right person as well. In other words, hiring is as much about *you* as it is about whom you hire.

Regardless of the circumstances you face, your attitude is one of the few things in life that is completely under your control. So, do you possess that necessary blend of energy, humor, compassion, team spirit, boldness, and initiative that you seek in others? Gutsy leaders understand that great people will go to work for really cool companies, but they will usually leave because of a bad boss. Would you hire you today?

Be Patient

After you reflect upon your attitude and feel clear about what you, as a boss, bring to the table, make a conscious decision to take your time during the hiring process. It's impossible to get to know someone in a few interviews, so be patient. Jeff Chambers, vice president of human resources at SAS, said, "I think we're still [hiring] the old-fashioned way. Our managers are looking for people who can have a long-term career with SAS because [we want to] . . . build long-term relationships with both our customers and our employees. A lot of managers hire so slow, it's almost like they're getting married to the person." Exactly!

That SAS's attrition has never been over 5 percent certainly validates the "old-fashioned way." Both its low attrition rate and the high rate at which clients renew their software licenses—98 percent—reflect SAS's success in establishing long-term relationships with employees and customers.

At SAS, it's not only HR and managers who make hiring decisions. It's a team process. If, say, a position for a senior developer became available, candidates would most likely have a group interview, the results of which would be passed on to the manager. Hiring decisions are team decisions. Said Suzanne Gordon, chief information officer and vice president of information technology for SAS, "We interview people to death. Although it's not a standardized process across the company, interviewing, especially for management-level positions, is both rigorous and time-consuming. The process includes meeting with people who will directly report to you, your supervisor, peers, and internal customers. It varies from place to place, but we . . . want to make sure that [potential hires will] fit and work well with everybody."

Real optimism is aware of problems but recognizes the solutions, knows about the difficulties but believes they can be overcome, sees the negatives but accentuates the positives, is exposed to the worst but expects the best, has reason to complain but chooses to smile.

—WILLIAM ARTHUR WARD

And guess what—it's the same with student positions. You'd think summer students coming from North Carolina State would be throwaways: Just get the bodies in, and if they don't work out, get rid of them at summer's end. Nope, SAS doesn't look at it that way. The company wants to hire students who can come in during the summer and then stay on during the school year, part-time. That way SAS can get a good look at their work ethic, their "fit" within the culture, assess their technical capabilities, and then, perhaps, make them an offer of full-time employment upon graduation. For SAS, it's a long-term perspective.

At a time when a lot of information-technology companies are laying people off, SAS is hiring. In 2000, it decided to increase its staff because Goodnight wanted to follow a hunch. He knew that "a lot of folks . . . are out on the street through no fault of their own. [They have been] . . . economic[ally] dislocat[ed]." Though they "would not typically look at SAS," they now notice "our model, our constant revenue growth and profitability, and our stability." SAS wanted to take advantage of this talent and grab these people while they were available. So, unlike the majority of other information-technology companies, SAS's staffing rose 8 percent in 2001 and 6 percent in 2002, and it is expected to rise again in 2003.

Back when the dot-coms were at their peak, SAS discovered a trend. Chambers remembered having people apply for positions who would say they were going to do all these great things. "It was all about them, them, them," he told us, "and what we're looking for is people who want to be a part of a larger community and want to contribute to something big. SAS isn't interested in people who are going to push, shove, and crawl their way to the top and grab the most that they can. People like that don't fit in."

SAS has built a culture of flexibility and trust. Chambers loves to use this example: If your daughter has a 3:00 P.M. soccer game, it's okay for you to leave and go to the game. Because at SAS it is assumed (you are trusted) that one of three things will happen. Either (A) you're going to get done what you have to get done before you leave, whether that means coming in early or working through lunch. Or (B) you're going to hand it off to a coworker, so the customer, the project, or whatever has to be done doesn't suffer. Or (C) you're going to log on from home later that evening and finish what you need to do. The company has never put a premium on face time, and it disdains micromanagers.

One way that SAS attracts top talent is by continually providing opportunities for people to create exotic software. The company puts 25 percent of its top-line money back into research and development every year, which is a significant investment in what highly skilled and extremely talented people value most—cool projects and cutting-edge technology. Chambers told us, "Our development talent loves that because they get to push the edge of the technology envelope every single day." They are generating energy and excitement that radiates throughout the entire organization. Everyone is enthusiastic about working on, testing, and selling advanced technology. What's more, the opportunity to contribute, add value, and make a difference is open to everyone in the company. No one is restricted because he or she is new or young.

SAS is an employer of choice because, according to Chambers, it "provide[s] a lot of flexibility so that people can balance work with life. . . . They get to work on cutting-edge technical projects, but they also get to have a life outside of work." The company's business model indicates that trusting your employees, and offering them flexible hours and exciting work, attracts highly talented, hardworking job applicants.

Culture Is a Hiring Tiebreaker

Again and again we were told the "right" culture acts as a magnet for the "right" talent and often serves as a valuable tiebreaker for candidates with more than one attractive offer. Jill Corsi, who joined USAA following a 16-year career in recruiting, told us, "USAA has an advantage in that we are an employer of choice, but we still have to determine if they are coming to USAA for the right reasons and [if we] are putting them in the right positions." A few years ago, Corsi remembers when she herself was interviewing for the job at USAA, she told people about her other job offers: "I would tell people I have an offer from company A and company B, and then [when] I'd say company C, USAA, people's faces would just light up, and these were people from all over the country. Now, I had no idea they were members or their cousin was a member or their sister was a member, but they'd just say, 'Oh, my gosh, that's the most fantastic company, you've got to go to work there.'" The brand, service, and culture were definitely a tiebreaker for Jill Corsi.

G U T S !

As GSD&M's Roy Spence discovered, one reason to hire great people is that they will hire other great people, who promote and protect GSD&M's culture with equal passion. And this is critical to Spence, because one visit to Idea City is all it takes to make people want to work there. Spence told us, "People fall in love with the spirit of this place. . . . When it comes to recruiting and winning in the talent game, culture is always our tiebreaker."

Similarly, Suzanne Gordon of SAS said, "We've been able to attract really good students that were being offered tremendous salaries [elsewhere] . . . but they just loved this culture so much that they stayed." There was another instance when Suzanne was trying to hire a developer from Seattle. Apparently, he looked really good on paper. When he went to SAS for the interviews, everyone really liked him, and by the time he got to Suzanne's office, he was convinced. "You know," he said, "I wasn't quite sure I wanted to move my family down from Seattle, but after talking to all the people and seeing how people work so well together and seeing this beautiful campus, I'm ready to sign up." There is no doubt that culture can be a powerful, competitive tool that will help you attract and hire the right kind of talent for your company.

Be Addicted to Great Talent

Regardless of the subject of their expertise, connoisseurs are more knowledgeable about wine, gourmet food, or fine art because of their passion for these things. If the subject is fine wine, they read the *Wine Spectator* and visit wineries to learn about harvesting grapes and the differences between vineyards. They attend wine-tasting events to learn about flavor. Connoisseurs talk with other connoisseurs about their collections, about new releases, and where to go for great buys. Many agree that the hunt for that special vintage can be addicting. Over time, they establish a powerful network of resources and accumulate a high level of knowledge. Why? Because they are simply more aggressive than others in the pursuit. The result? They are usually able to find the best wine at the best price in the shortest amount of time.

We have two friends who are connoisseurs of world-class talent: Kevin Towers, general manager, and Bruce Bochy, manager, of the San Diego Padres. Kevin's success is determined by his ability to recruit the best ballplayers, and Bruce's success depends on his ability to develop those players. Constrained by a small-cap market with a lower-than-average payroll, these men live, eat, and breathe the pursuit of great baseball talent. Why? Because the success of the team and their livelihood depend on it. Those same reasons should be motivating you in your pursuit of great talent.

When you're working with business-intelligence software, it seems obvious that you've got to hire some very intelligent people. But SAS doesn't restrict its search to brainpower alone. It also looks for enthusiasm and persistence. "A lot of intelligent people just quit the first time they hit a roadblock," Suzanne Gordon said. "I always look for people that won't take no for an answer and are persistent in pursuing whatever it is that they're good at. We also want people who . . . communicate well, motivate others, and don't come across as a technology snob."

Like GSD&M, SAS values a strong work ethic. Gordon told us, "There are nice benefits, but, in exchange for those nice benefits, you're expected to work hard, and people do work really hard here. And it's a big part of their life."

It's not an exaggeration to say that SAS's Jim Goodnight is addicted to great talent. So, when Gordon finds it but doesn't actually have an open position, she makes it a priority to bump into Goodnight. A number of years ago, SAS hired a student intern from North Carolina State who, according to those with whom she worked, was highly talented and brilliant. Gordon didn't want to lose her, but she didn't have a full-time position to offer her. She invited the gifted intern to lunch, hoping to bump into Goodnight, which they did at the salad bar. Gordon recalled, "I introduced her and explained [to Goodnight] how good she was, but that I didn't have an open position and thought he might know about another position on campus." After talking with her, Goodnight said: "Oh, go ahead, fill out a hiring requisition. I'll sign it." Gordon confessed to using that strategy on more than one occasion. "I knew if Dr. Goodnight met them and saw how bright they were," she said, "he wouldn't want to lose them either."

Gordon mentioned another particularly brilliant intern who told her that a piece of software that Goodnight had written should work differently. The next time Gordon saw Dr. Goodnight, she told him about the student. Eventually, the intern sat down with the chairman, and after their conversation, he offered the intern a full-time position.

We heard it over and over again in different ways at SAS: Talented people are our competitive edge, and we're committed to doing whatever it takes to find, recruit, and retain them. The SAS community networks intensively to build and protect its culture of intelligence.

Everyone Is Responsible for Hiring

At places like SAS, GSD&M, Planet Honda, USAA, and Semco, everyone plays a role in hiring. In the long run, the goal of hiring is not only to fill an open position, but to build a community of talent. Suzanne Gordon remembers plowing through a pile of résumés and calling the candidate who seemed best for a particular job, one Scott Van Valkenburgh. The rapport was instant, and the two talked for more than an hour on the phone. After she interviewed him in person and he was interviewed by the team, everyone was in agreement:

Scott was perfect for the job and for SAS. Gordon was delighted, and brought Scott to meet her boss. Suddenly, the ground shifted under her. "After talking with Scott," she said, "my boss called me and said, 'Suzanne, this guy is great. You did an excellent job finding him. But you can't have him, because he is perfect for another open position we have.' I was disappointed, but his experience did fit my boss's open position perfectly, so I was okay with it. I figured at least we would get Scott at SAS. I think that is one of the big things we try to do at SAS. We don't concentrate so much on our own area, but instead on what is good for SAS overall."

Hire Renegades and Revolutionaries

In a world moving at Internet speed, with ever-more-demanding customers insisting on greater convenience and customization, innovation is clearly key to survival. The trouble is, the creative people we need to meet those demands often turn out to be wild-eyed, emotional, volatile, and unpredictable individuals. You might feel hesitant to hire them, but changing old-fashioned habits, breaking the chains of bureaucracy, and liberating your organization from ideas of the past that no longer work all require fiercely determined people willing to take risks. In most organizations, the concept of "business as usual" is a formidable adversary, particularly adept at protecting itself. If you want to change your company radically, sometimes you need to bring in a new breed of revolutionaries. Unique, passionate, and full of "crazy" ideas, such individuals are bent on making their mark, and most likely they will.

Some of the greatest innovators and agents of change in the world were considered radical members of the counterculture—irreverent, impatient, disruptive, and fanatical. As the cliché goes, where would we be without them, socially, spiritually, politically, and economically? Still, it often feels too risky to have them working for us.

It takes guts to hire people who are different from you. The tendency for most of us is to hire in our own image, because doing so makes us feel comfortable and lets us avoid all sorts of challenges and difficulties in our relationships. However, mirror-image hiring breeds insulated and cloistered businesses—and, most important, robs us of the gifts that mavericks bring. It is such fresh perspectives, new ideas, better ways of working, and breakthrough innovations that truly differentiate a company from its competition.

Don't misunderstand us. You should, of course, continue to hire for cultural fit; that's absolutely necessary. But be careful not to confuse unity with uniformity. A united culture is a harmonious one that is open to "difference." Planet Honda has a broad spectrum of

A **uniform culture,** in which everyone is the same, **will suffocate innovation**.

employees who speak 15 different languages, yet they are all united around the same cultural imperatives. At GSD&M's Idea City, people of different ages, ethnicities, personalities, and political beliefs are united in their passionate focus on building brands of purpose, and in their commitment to the values driving the agency. They are united around a heroic cause and a common set of ideals within which they can unleash their creativity. A uniform culture, in which everyone is the same, will suffocate innovation.

Though renegades, rebels, and rule breakers can create confusion and chaos, they also keep the fires of passion stoked and the waters of creativity stirred. They bring vibrancy, initiative, and an appetite for adventure that inspire other employees to greater achievement. The question facing companies becomes: Should our passion for innovation override whatever fears and insecurities we have about hiring people who are different from us?

Given the unorthodox way Semco is run, what is the secret behind Ricardo Semler's success? Hire people who act like adults and be radical about giving them the freedom to do their jobs. In his book *The Seven-Day Weekend,* Semler said, "We think 20 to 30 percent of everybody's time in business is concerned with boarding-school issues—when do you come in, what are you called, what are you paid, whom can you talk to, and what can you say to them? It's a hell of a lot of time. We're liberating people." In an environment in which power is delegated and trust is assumed, peer pressure keeps everyone performing at his or her highest capacity. "It's as [close to a] free market as we can make it. People bring their talents, and we rely on their self-interest to use the company to develop themselves in any way they see fit," Semler explained. "In return, they must have the self-discipline to perform."

Even though the few offices that exist are equipped with hammocks for afternoon naps, Semco may not be the worker's paradise that it sounds like. People who don't perform have a difficult time

If employees treat **the company** as though it's **their own**, it naturally follows that they should **decide what it will become**.

hiding. To stay at Semco, a manager has to choose you as someone he or she will need for the next six months. So you are constantly updating your portfolio and building your brand within the company. Those who add value "re-up," whereas those who don't, leave. "Freedom is no easy thing," said Semler. Instead of "making life carefree . . . it introduces difficult choices."

Only people with certain attitudes will succeed in a culture where self-discipline replaces top-down enforcement and control. For example, someone who seeks approval from big titles, works hard only to please others, or has trouble assuming responsibility will be crushed at Semco. This company attracts people who trust their own instincts (go with their gut) and believe that the only genuine source of authority comes from within themselves. Survival is not in the hands of others; it's in their own hands. If employees treat the company as though it's their own, it naturally follows that they should decide what it will become.

Conventional companies believe that the most trusted sources of knowledge are those who set strategy and have a larger perspective. Needless to say, power and control reside with them. Consequently, as we know, success is defined by moving up the corporate ladder, not by making valued contributions. This view assumes that if employees are not tightly controlled, they will act against the company's best interest. To avoid that, a tight command-and-control system is put in place. But beware, it can suck the life out of your organization.

Ricardo Semler's unorthodox approach is based on an antithetical worldview. He believes that people will act responsibly and in their own best interests, which are intricately tied to those of the company. He encourages his employees to make strong commitments to what they are most happy doing. While working at what they enjoy and believe in, they will place more stringent demands on themselves than any authority figure could. Semler's attitude is that when people are free to do what they enjoy, their successes will far outnumber their failures. Besides, what pumps their adrenaline will also make money.

Semco is alive with passion, energy, and excitement because it looks for and finds people who are not afraid to express themselves. To succeed in this radical culture, you must have the courage to take risks and talk straight, letting others know where you stand. You gain influence and power by having good ideas, constructive debates, and authentic dialogues with your peers—not by reason of your position or title. Without freedom of expression, you have a dull, gray, boring bureaucracy with no competitive advantage. According to Semler, "It's easy to get a sizable organization to change without telling it to, provided you are willing to give up labels, boundaries, and restrictions."

Semler is not alone in his type of "madness." At the Whole Foods chain, hiring is left completely in local hands. Store leaders screen candidates, then recommend them for a job on a specific team. And only teams have the power to approve new members. It takes a two-thirds vote of the team after what is usually a 30-day trial period before the candidate can be officially hired.

This peer hiring process has been a real boon to Whole Foods. It takes ownership out of the realm of the abstract; it is empowerment at large, because people have some real control over their work lives. Leaders, all the way up to John Mackey, its chief executive, are never alarmed when a candidate is rejected. On the contrary, they take it as proof of commitment. "When you have a team saying 'no' to someone, they're also saying 'yes' to themselves," said Mackey. "'Yes, we have high standards, and we're not going to let anyone jeopardize them.' There's a tremendous sense of ownership that comes with that."

Like Semco, Whole Foods offers another important incentive for teams to hire only stellar candidates: their own bottom line. Under the Whole Foods gain-sharing program, bonuses are directly linked to a team's performance. Accept a slacker on your team, and you may actually lose money. How's that for blowing the doors off business as usual?

Acknowledge Your New Hires

When great people join an organization, what information do they want immediately? They want to know if they made the right decision. And they want to know what's expected of them and what it will take to fit in. Some smart companies seek to lessen new hires' concerns by addressing them instantly. Your best bet is to celebrate the arrival of new people. You never get a second chance to make a great first impression.

Planet Honda's treatment of new people is intended to help them feel welcome, capable, and confident with the company's way of doing things as quickly as possible. Its mantra—"Knowledge breeds confidence, confidence breeds enthusiasm, and enthusiasm sells"—tells you right away what is expected and how to fit in. Ciasulli takes

When people are **free** to do what they enjoy, their **successes** will far **outnumber their failures**.

training seriously; as a result, every new person attends an orientation called Planet 101. Included in the program are a tour of each department, an in-depth description of the company's culture and character, and two weeks of intensive training that immerses them in Planet Honda's culture, processes, and procedures. For example, sales training includes shadowing a pro within the dealership, who both explains and demonstrates the nuances of Planet Honda's approach. Next, new hires demonstrate what they have learned while being videotaped. This can be very helpful. By replaying the video, for example, they are able to spot weaknesses—for example, talking so fast that they skip steps in a sales presentation.

Ciasulli wants every salesperson to be able to work a deal from start to finish. This means they need to know how to move a customer from a purchase option to a lease option and vice versa, how to calculate payments quickly, and how to demonstrate the product inside and out. All that may seem obvious, but this level of training is unprecedented in the industry. And it works because knowledge-

The most important measure of how good of a game I played was how much better I made my teammates play.

—BILL RUSSELL

able people exude a depth of confidence that invites customers to trust them.

At Stanley Steemer, the Dublin, Ohio–based carpet-cleaning giant, new hires are not oriented or trained right away; instead they are celebrated.

Founded in 1947, this company began just as wall-to-wall carpeting was starting to roll across America's floors. By now, the business has grown to more than 230 franchises.

Phil Dean, one of Stanley's gutsy leaders, is a perceptive straight shooter who understands his recruits' attitudes and emotions. He knows that the company doesn't "attract rocket scientists. . . . It's not that hard to learn how to clean carpets. But that doesn't mean these folks don't want to better themselves and their families. We tell them they're joining an organization that's dedicated to helping them make their dreams come true."

By and large, the company hires males fresh out of high school, whose minds are filled with what Dean calls "the head trash" of adolescent experiences: low grades, the loss of college-bound friends, failure to make the football team, romantic defeats, and their inability to get more than entry-level jobs. Unsurprisingly, they feel like

"We put as much **effort into attitude** as we do into **aptitude.**"

losers. "Our orientation teaches them to clean carpets," Dean said, "but its central mission is to convince them that they can be winners. We put as much effort into attitude as we do into aptitude."

At Stanley, each new person is given a "passport," which lists eight top executives with whom the employee must meet and discuss the company. At the end of each appointment, the executive signs the passport. The system tells the recruits that they are worth the time and attention of top management—and, at the same time, it reminds the executives of their commitment to helping every employee feel important.

After their first month, the new hires, in groups of three or four, spend six hours with Dean and his wife. The sessions start with a two-hour, wide-ranging discussion of everyone's values, goals, and dreams. The Deans strive to create a safe, comfortable environment where everyone feels secure enough to confide in the group. Then a pile of magazines, glue sticks, scissors, and poster board are brought out, and the whole group, including the Deans, builds "dream boards." Collages made up of pictures cut from the magazines, they represent each person's goals, hopes, and even undeveloped yearnings. There might be a photo of a rap artist driving a Rolls-Royce; a cozy cabin nestled among trees; or a man tutoring a disadvantaged child. The dream boards are sized to fit on the inside door of each employee's locker, where they will serve as daily reminders that this Stanley Steemer franchise encourages dreams. And when they finish, the Deans lead a four-hour discussion of how the organization can help make each worker's dreams come true.

The dream boards offer remarkable psychological insight (you become what you think about) and show profound caring on the part of Stanley Steemer. This technique could be successful for you, too. But you've got to care as passionately as the Deans do.

A lot to think about? Absolutely. But if you want to pare down the hiring concept, simply remember this: Avoid people who suck. Instead, hire and keep people who have the ability and desire to inspire others to achieve higher levels of commitment, energy, and productivity. Your effort will be richly repaid. Then, and only then, will you be positioned to blow the dusty ledgers off of business-as-usual.

You become what you think about.

✓ **Ready, aim, fire:** Your first step in the hiring process is to identify the abilities and attitudes you want a new employee to have. Of course, you need to understand what his or her specific tasks will be, but also be clear on what sort of personality will help you establish or enhance your culture's brand from the inside. Hiring a very capable person whose style and character clash with the company's values is a mistake; so is hiring someone whose personality is "a perfect fit" but who is not a top performer.

✓ **Make talent a strategic priority:** Do what GSD&M and General Electric have done: Move hiring to the level of strategy. Your executive team should be involved in recruiting and retaining world-class talent. Jack Welch created enviable "bench strength" during his tenure at GE. He was intimately involved with recruiting and hiring for the top 500 positions at GE. Once Jeff Immelt was chosen to succeed Welch, the next two executives in line for the top job were immediately offered CEO positions by IBM and Home Depot.

Hold a symposium twice a year in which your leaders identify the best recruitment and retention practices in your organization. Determine the relationship between the recruiting initiatives and retention rates. Measure the "bench strength" of every leader in your organization and base part of his or her compensation on the results.

✓ **Develop a profile:** One of the tricks to hiring the best is knowing what they look like. Start by identifying your best employees, then ask their customers, employees, peers, and managers to explain what makes them so effective and easy to work with. Discover how they help their teammates develop, how they interact with colleagues, respond to the needs of customers, and get results. Examine their skills and performance history, considering unconventional traits, such as sense of humor, grace under pressure, purpose and dedication, and confidence. Make sure to involve the team that the new hire will join. It needs to be heard regarding what it wants and needs in a new member.

Based on what you learn, establish a profile that highlights the attributes that these winners share. Draft interview questions designed to screen specifically for these characteristics, including the ability to blend well with this group and a positive, optimistic outlook. Know the attitudes you are looking for and don't compromise.

✓ **What people know is less important than who they are:** What kind of person do you want working with you? Of course, he or she must be knowledgeable, but not at the price of an incompatible attitude—don't ever assume that will change. You can teach someone your systems and methodologies, but not how to collaborate or how to fit into a culture whose values she or he doesn't share.

✓ **Hire for purpose:** Learn from Roy Spence and Tim Ciasulli: Look for people who want their work to make a difference. A résumé that looks "too good to be true" may belong to someone who feels he or she has "arrived" in his or her career and wants to continue doing exactly what got him or her there. That's bad news if your business demands ongoing innovation. What you want in your organization is the right combination of talent, moxie, imagination, dreams, energy, and drive. Pedestals are for leaping from, not resting on.

✓ **Hire the unconventional:** People who think, act, and approach critical issues from the same perspective will eventually create an atmosphere of homogeneity that deadens the organization. Then, when circumstances or the environment change, as they inevitably will, the organization is incapable of reacting rapidly and effectively. Look for open-minded people who are fun, spontaneous, and have the guts to take a risk—people who will help you transcend boundaries, even when doing so makes you slightly uncomfortable.

✓ **Screen for passion:** Don't be put off by gaps in a résumé's timeline. They may reflect independent thinking. Also, you don't want someone whose path in life is too neat, too orderly, too predictable. Since people are always on their best behavior during job interviews, the way to screen for passion is to encourage the applicant to discuss spontaneously his or her past accomplishments, choices, passions, and hobbies. Listen not only for the content, but for the tone, the enthusiasm, and the passion.

Every organization should have a series of interview questions geared to its specific needs, but here are a few that may stimulate your thinking when screening for ideas and attitudes:

- When was the last time you broke the rules to serve a customer?
- Tell me about a time when you went out of your way to meet a customer's need.

- Have you ever used humor to diffuse a tense situation? When? How?
- Was there ever a time when you went beyond the call of duty to assist a coworker without claiming credit? When? How?
- When was the last time you tried something new? When did you last volunteer to assume additional responsibility?
- When was the last time you sought feedback on your performance?
- Have you received negative feedback lately? Did you agree? How did you respond?
- What have you learned in the last three weeks that could add new value to your organization?
- Describe a time when working on a team proved more successful than working on your own.

✓ Hire people who are good at what you aren't:

Gutsy leaders are in touch with their weaknesses and look for people who can compensate for them. If the San Diego Padres have a weak bullpen, they hire a stellar relief pitcher. If they have a low-scoring season, they search for a home-run hitter. You want to cultivate an approach that celebrates your strengths but acknowledges and balances your weaknesses. Gutsy leaders put their egos aside. They understand their own weaknesses, and they aren't afraid to surround themselves with people who have strengths that they don't.

✓ Win the war for talent in every community you serve:

Although we might like to believe that with appropriate training and encouragement everyone can excel, the fact remains that one really talented employee is worth a dozen mediocre ones. We agree with *Good to Great* author Jim Collins, who believes that the only difference between a good company and one that's great is the quality of its talent.

Nothing is more important to gutsy leaders than finding and recruiting the right talent.

✓ Market your open positions creatively: Your marketing campaign must be tailored to match the specific skills and attitudes you're seeking. If you are trying to hire imaginative individuals with initiative and verve, you want your message to reflect that. No one is better at this than Southwest Airlines. One of its recruitment ads featured a child's scribbled drawing and a teacher admonishing Brian to "please try to color inside the lines!" The caption read: "Brian shows an early aptitude for working at Southwest Airlines." Another ad, featuring a Lyle Lovett look-alike, read, "At Southwest, we don't care if you have big hair [and] sing off key, all we ask is that you take your job and LUV it!" Capturing your attention, these ads make you smile and, most important, attract precisely the kind of people Southwest wants. Ask yourself if your recruitment campaign does the same, and if it doesn't, try to craft ads that creatively reflect your style, brand, and culture.

✓ Don't limit your talent search to the usual channels: Be gutsy, be fearless! As Roy Spence pointed out, most world-class talent is already employed, so you may have to take risks to find new, creative means to capture them. Here are some suggestions:

• Attend conferences with the sole intent of recruiting. Ask board members, program chairs, and officers for the names of superstars. Look at the meeting's agenda, then initiate a conversation and establish a relationship with the speaker. Ask him or her for tips on hot talent. If you lead a seminar or are a member of a panel, keep a vigil for articulate, interesting participants.

• Read trade journals. Find out who is writing and making significant contributions in your field. Begin a dialogue with them. After all, you never know where such a conversation could lead. Ask journal editors who has caught their attention.

• Read the newspaper with the outlook that the names of shakers and movers often appear in press releases and articles; listen to radio and television interviews with the same goal. Notice who is quoted, and in what context. The point is to keep your antennae bristling for any sound of talent.

• Keep this priority in mind: The next time you receive excellent service from someone, offer a business card and ask the person to call you if he or she would like to explore a new opportunity. You may find a talented soul yearning for a new chapter in life.

• Consult with every new hire; ask for the names of a few superstars in the industry or at their previous company. Also, ask about gutsy leaders, mentors, coaches, and consultants who have impressed them in the past.

• Tap the knowledge and experience of consultants; having worked with many people, they can often point you in the direction of a superstar.

• Use the Web and watch for people with exciting Web sites. The Internet is the new medium for authentic expression and gives you access to frank conversations on products, services, and even the reputations of people in your field. Names that come up in chat room discussions are worth noting.

✓ **Turn everyone into a recruiter:** Gallup's research shows that having a friend at work ranks higher than pay, benefits, and promotions as a factor that influences the degree to which workers are committed to their jobs. Hence, ask your great people if they have friends who would also "fit" well into your company. It's a strategy that works for SAS; let it work for you, too.

✓ **Trust your gut!** Remember, you need to **hire people** you **enjoy** being around. If you don't feel a particular person **"fits" well in your culture,** trust your **instincts** and do not compromise.

✓ **Let the team decide:** Don't let the human-resources department hire for you. HR can be very helpful in conducting the initial screening, but it should not make the final cut. Take a page from SAS's playbook and let the team decide. In addition, get feedback from a customer group that will work directly with the new hire.

✓ **Fire for attitude:** Phil Dean of Stanley Steemer knows that, like an untreated cancer, one employee's bad attitude can spread to an entire team. While we are focusing on avoiding this problem by hiring the right people, gutsy leaders have to be ruthless about protecting their enterprises from destructive influences that surface from within. We have all had to deal with unhappy people whose personal misery interferes with their ability to work well. Their pessimism stifles initiative, curbs enthusiasm, and shatters team spirit.

✓ **Hire for fit:** Though rarely acknowledged in business, it is a fact that interpersonal "chemistry" is a prerequisite for success. Simply put, people who get along and like each other perform better. A successful team almost always produces its own synergy that transcends the immediate work project.

✓ Re-recruiting and keeping your great people:

Keeping great people requires re-recruiting them, and that means finding ways to keep them happy. Routinely, gutsy leaders treat their best people as though they were constantly being wooed by another company. Of course, this means paying competitive wages, but praising, recognizing, and celebrating your people's contributions are crucial. Harvard Business School's Rosabeth Moss Kanter wrote, "Compensation is a right, recognition is a gift"; Wal-Mart's Sam Walton said, "Outstanding leaders go out of their way to boost the self-esteem of their people. If people believe in themselves, it's amazing what they can accomplish."

How to do that: Successful companies constantly provide their most-prized people with compelling reasons to stay. Promotions, challenging assignments, public recognition, mentoring, and personal time with senior management are just a few. Another, paradoxically, is making sure that your superstars continuously enhance their own marketability. Jack Welch became famous for developing his people to such an extent that they were always being recruited by GE's competitors. But, unlike GE, most organizations don't have an endless supply of great talent, and the real goal is to keep who they have. Southwest Airlines has a unique twist on GE's formula: It encourages its departments to woo superstars away from their departments and into others. Al Davis, head of internal auditing, said his turnover rate has been as high as 50 percent as a result of internal transfers. When you facilitate people's marketability, they don't generally leave; instead, they stay and offer more value to your company.

Here are suggestions for a plan aimed at retaining and re-recruiting great people. Start by establishing a team with a mandate of creating 25 meaningful ways to hold on to your people.

1. Are your leaders people whom others want to follow? Are they fun to work with? Are they dedicated to the success of others? Do they support their people? Do your leaders help people realize that they are truly valued? Are they active, engaged listeners? What can leaders do to improve these or other aspects of their relationships with their people?

2. Give your valued people cool projects. Will those being worked on today be remembered in five years? Does their work stretch people and enhance their skills? Do the projects you assign enhance their marketability? Can you reframe or redefine projects so that everyone will feel passionate about them?

3. Allow people to feel emotionally attached to the company, which happens when they feel appreciated for their contributions. Do you have reward and recognition programs that ensure that? Do these programs reinforce the values that drive your business? Do they affirm the specific attitudes and behaviors you expect from your people? Try to provide spontaneous as well as formal events that show people how much you appreciate them.

4. Help people develop self-confidence. Insecurity can manifest in a resistance to change and can lead to power struggles and turf battles. Give your people challenging, meaningful assignments at which they can succeed, but don't punish failure. Taking risks should be rewarded.

5. Find ways to review the organization's mission, vision, and values. Sharing and embracing them will help people develop a strong, self-sustaining corporate culture to which everyone will feel dedicated.

6. Jettison the bureaucracy and shrink your headquarters. How many people are actually required to sign off before a junior employee can act? Reduce the hierarchy to no more than three or four levels.

7. Practice informal, direct, and immediate ways of communicating. If something can be decided upon by a handshake in the hallway, instead of a meeting or a full-scale report, use the handshake.

8. Eliminate tribalism. Give people diverse, cross-functional experience; doing so will help them empathize with their coworkers' jobs and breed team spirit.

9. Get rid of the jobs that distract people. Ask people what they are ignoring because they are distracted by other required tasks. What takes them away from the work that truly adds value for your customers and creates competitive advantage for your company?

What **compelling reason** are you **giving** your **people to stay?**

CHAPTER 5

Gutsy Leaders
Lead with Love

During some heavy ice storms in upstate New York, Stephanie Valdez, a representative of USAA, the financial-services company, received a call from a Mrs. Lawless, the elderly widow of a deceased military officer. Mrs. Lawless told Valdez that she was sick, without her medicine, and as if that weren't enough, she had no heat and was nearly freezing. She explained that her husband had a USAA insurance policy and had instructed her that if she ever had a problem and didn't know where else to turn, she should call USAA. "He said you would take care of me," she concluded.

Love is a Choice

When Valdez retrieved the records, she discovered that the policy hadn't been maintained since the officer's death. But that didn't stop Valdez, who put her former client on hold and called the Red Cross. That afternoon, Mrs. Lawless got her medicine and the heat was restored in her home. Mr. Lawless had told his wife that USAA would take care of her when no one else could, and Valdez was determined to make good on that promise, whether the premiums were paid or not.

Unlike most companies, USAA is not just focused on training people to adhere to the guidelines of a "policy." Its employees want to be safe havens for their customers, whom they refer to as "members." Serving people connected to the military, USAA's appreciation of its members is steadfast and sincere. Repeatedly, people in every position in the company told us they feel that "it's a privilege to serve those who do so much for our country."

And members of the military respond with enthusiasm. The organization has $66 billion in owned and managed assets and more than 21,000 employees. Today, 96 percent of active-duty U.S. military officers and 44 percent of active-duty noncommissioned officers have chosen to be USAA members. The company also insures astronauts, the only organization to do so. Talk about a niche market.

When we ask members of our audiences all over the world how many are insured with USAA, there are always raised hands. When we ask if any would be willing to switch insurance companies, the response is always an emphatic "No!" With very little advertising, USAA's total revenues add up to $9 billion annually; its member-retention rate is more than 96 percent, and much of its business comes from word of mouth.

The important question is Why does USAA deserve 95 percent of its market? For starters, it doesn't sell its members anything they don't need. It leverages technology to make it extremely convenient for members to do business with the company, and it frequently

LOYALTY

"Loyalty goes both ways—whether it's family, country, work, or anything else. It means sharing dedication, commitment, and dependability. I've been married to the same man for 36 years, attended the same church for 33, worked for the same company for 40, and been an American through it all."
— Alice Kalinoski, USAA employee since 1962, member since 1968

exceeds its members' expectations. Bob Davis, chairman and chief executive officer, believes that it is because the company is committed to maintaining a sacred trust between USAA and its members. Davis told us that "what we have is a connection that no other company has." He continued, "As a member, I never worried about [insurance issues] when I was in Vietnam, because my wife always knew to call USAA if anything went wrong. . . . It's like a marriage: The most important thing is trust, and we can never ever violate [it]. . . . If we do, it's over."

When love and skill work together, expect a miracle.

—JOHN RUSKIN

We realized quickly that what Bob Davis means by "connection" is, in fact, the company's love for members of the collective military family. When the first Gulf War broke out, USAA generated a list of all members who were on duty in the Middle East. When the troops came home, it sent a letter to them all, expressing the company's pride and appreciation for everything they did for our country, and welcoming them home safely. Attached was a premium refund for the entire time they were serving in the Gulf, because, as the letter essentially said, "we figured you weren't driving your car too much."

How did USAA get that way? It started in 1922 when 26 U.S. Army officers met in a hotel in San Antonio, Texas, and put together an auto-insurance association. Because they moved around a lot, they had been labeled "transients" by most car-insurance companies and denied coverage. They welcomed Marine and Navy officers to the club in 1924 and adopted the name United Services Automobile Association.

As the number of members increased, USAA expanded into just about every variety of insurance, including property-and-casualty and life insurance. Now it offers members a complete financial package—banking, discount brokerage, financial planning, mutual funds, real-estate investments, and overall retirement and investment planning. Finance aside, USAA has leveraged its growing membership rolls—5 million at last count—by introducing a discount purchasing program and a mail-order catalog business, not to mention its long-distance telephone and credit-card operations. The company started enrolling enlisted personnel in 1997.

All through the years, USAA has been a pioneer in adopting new technologies. It was one of the first insurance companies to change from mail to toll-free telephone numbers, and by the late 1980s it was using an optical storage system to automate some operations. A few years later, it adopted advanced screen telephones to create a home banking system.

Along with most organizations, USAA found its investment income drastically reduced during the millennial recession. It was forced to lay off workers in 2000 for the first time ever, and its $500 million net in 2002 was a drop from previous years. But the loyalty of its members is USAA's key asset, and the company predicts a doubling of its membership by 2010.

Have the Guts to Love

In some circles, love is considered unbusinesslike—an amorphous concept that may be appropriate only in the professional lives of nurses, physicians, social workers, and teachers. Clearly, in this view, love doesn't belong in a big brawny business. We disagree. Inherent in the human condition is the need to be loved, to be cared for, and why would we think that need evaporates when we enter the workplace? In fact, it doesn't make sense to expect your employees to function effectively in an environment that doesn't acknowledge their psychological or emotional needs.

Inherent in the **human condition** is the **need to be loved**.

This concept applies to customers as well as employees. People want to conduct business with companies that care about them as individuals as opposed to objectified market segments. We believe that there's a place for such caring, for—dare we say it?—love in business. Certainly, we aren't proposing that your company become a social-service agency. We're suggesting that you acknowledge compassion for and concern for others as a valuable business asset.

Trish Derho, the infamous marketing queen of our Freibergs.com, once said, "I work better when I'm loved. Try it!" Maybe we should all try it? People act differently, less defensively, when they feel loved.

Employees are willing to be more flexible, more accountable, when they're drawn by love rather than driven by fear. Customers will become passionately devoted to your company if your ambassadors genuinely care about them.

Why, then, are so many business leaders reluctant to express love, to genuinely care for one another, at work? Perhaps they fear being viewed as soft-hearted romantics instead of hard-headed realists. Maybe they equate love with self-indulgent, nonbusinesslike behavior. Yet neither is the case in the organizations we studied. More than an intermittent sentiment, love is gutsy, a decision of the will made out of an altruistic commitment to the well-being of others, even when such a decision is inconvenient or even costly. Gutsy leaders choose to love even when they don't feel like it.

Rising above self-interest requires a strong will, discipline, and a sense of security that not everyone can pull off. It takes guts, for instance, to tell people the truth about their rough edges in a performance review because you want them to succeed. Taking a risk and "going to bat" for someone with the boss may be politically incorrect, but it also may be the right thing to do.

Acting out of genuine concern for other people is gutsy because it often asks us to do what may be uncomfortable or counterintuitive. It asks us at times to take a stand on issues that may not be in our personal interest, as well as to be open and vulnerable. If I leave a meeting in which my manager was unreasonable, I can either complain about him or her to my colleagues, or I can request another meeting to work out the problem behind closed doors. The latter is the smarter—and more diplomatic—choice. The former can lead to tribalism (discussed in Chapter 2) and only makes for a toxic work environment. My manager also has a choice. While he or she may not feel apologetic, the response that shows a genuine concern for my feelings is to admit that he or she can see things from my point of view. We can wallow in defensiveness, denial, and self-pity, or we can transcend the moment and act in accordance with the more charitable values by which most of us live.

"Love" Is Good Business

Southwest's Herb Kelleher expressed this idea well: "I'd rather have a company bound by love than a company bound by fear." This isn't just the worldview of an Irishman known for his demonstrative displays of affection. Herb understands the business argument for a culture "bound by love." Employees working at companies that care about them are far more than satisfied—they are engaged, loyal, and fully committed to the organization with their minds and their

Gutsy leaders **choose to love** even **when they don't feel like it**.

hearts. Such organizations are much more likely to attract and retain world-class talent, and their employees are far more likely to perform at higher levels of commitment and productivity, which helps create loyal customers and increase profitability.

Most of the gutsy leaders we came across—including those highlighted in this book—would not describe their recipes for success as "love." Yet all would point to critical ingredients that characterize an organization that is, in Herb Kelleher's phrase, bound by love. Here are examples of such acts of kindness and caring within a business environment.

Know the Person Behind the Customer

USAA's Bob Davis knows it is virtually impossible to serve people well if you're unfamiliar with their needs and lifestyles. As a result, his company goes to great lengths to help employees identify with their members. Every month, Davis holds a meeting with all of the company's managers that is broadcast via satellite to all employees of the organization.

Vicki Mcbride, a forty-four-year employee, receives a dozen yellow roses and applause from CEO Bob Davis on her last day with USAA.

One of the meeting's highlights is a member video profile that describes the member's daily family life as accurately as possible. Davis, whose father was a U.S. Navy officer, was drafted into the Army and was eventually promoted to captain before he left the service. He is the most highly decorated combat veteran to have ever led USAA. Having experienced many of the significant events that are unique to the military, Davis has shared the passions and felt the concerns of his USAA members. He's adamant about his employees' understanding the impact of military life on members' lives and how it indelibly defines their identities. That's why he has gone to the trouble of discussing member profiles. He realizes how crucial it is that his employees make a connection with USAA members. "You can't just tell someone about this," Davis said. "They have to see it, feel it, and become a part of it."

The profile we watched when we visited USAA was the deployment of the USS *Constellation* out of San Diego. Sailors worried about leaving their families for six months. Who would handle their finances? One fighter pilot looked down from the aircraft's deck as his wife stood on the pier holding their young daughter. Tears were flowing as sailors and their families and loved ones waved goodbye and held hand-lettered signs reading, "We Miss You" and "I Love You." It seemed obvious that, for most of these sailors, this parting would be among the hardest things they would ever do.

photo: Eric Myer

How could USAA make it easier? How could the company help? USAA celebrates Memorial Day and Veterans Day by inviting military commanders and senior noncommissioned officers to a ceremony that honors the sacrifices military men and women have made for the country. Recently, the company invited a noncommissioned

"I'd **rather** have a company **bound by love than** a company bound **by fear**."

officer from the Air Force special-operations command to address USAA employees. With his wife and new baby at his side, he told of riding out on horseback to locate enemy caves and bunkers in Afghanistan, leaving his unit behind, and of his return to find that his unit had been decimated in a bombing.

Listening to such experiences is one way in which Davis challenges his employees. "You have to look your members in the eye," he told us, and "love those people who are . . . serving and taking care of us every day." The member profile is designed to personify the member on the other end of the phone line; the recipient of the letter you're writing; or the reader of the company's magazines.

It takes a special effort to identify with an 18- or 20-year-old new mother who has become a parent virtually overnight and doesn't know if her husband will ever come home alive. Davis believes that if USAA's people are empathetic and able to personally connect with members, extraordinary acts of service will follow.

Let People See They Can Trust You

The bond between USAA and its members reflects trust in a military culture in which the stakes are literally life and death. General Bill Cooney, USAA's legendary former vice chairman, gave this simple example: "If you tell me you're going to be over Bosnia at a certain time and place, you had better be there, because I'm counting on you. If you're not there, I could be dead." What Cooney expressed is the exquisitely heightened expectation that people will look out for each other. And USAA has shown itself worthy of such trust more than once.

For example, Jim Middleton, president and chief executive of USAA Life Insurance Company, told us that in July 2001, Deborah Patterson, an employee in USAA's property-and-casualty business, suggested to a member who worked at the World Trade Center in New York that he consider life insurance. The member agreed. He began the application process, and by September the contract, including blood tests and medical examinations, had been completed. All he had to do was pay his first month's premium. Then, on September 11, 2001, two planes crashed into the World Trade Center and the member was killed. USAA immediately sent a crisis-response team to Ground Zero.

Among the first people the USAA team encountered at the crisis operations center was this member's widow. In the mayhem of the tragedy, she remembered that her husband had a life-insurance policy pending with USAA. Reminiscent of how Stephanie Valdez handled Mrs. Lawless and owing to the tragic and highly unusual circumstances, USAA accepted the first month's payment from the member's wife and paid off the $125,000 policy. Jim Middleton told us that he "would do it again in a minute."

USAA is blowing the papers off insurance-as-usual by taking the opposite approach. During the war with Iraq, the United States deployed more than 225,000 troops to the Middle East, and USAA continued to stand behind each and every member. In addition to SGLI, a Serviceman's Group Life Insurance policy worth $250,000, and to which every member of the armed services is now entitled, USAA is offering an additional $250,000, bringing the total life coverage to $500,000 with no additional blood tests or medical exams.

A few years ago, after Kevin praised USAA's virtues in a presentation, a member in the audience shared a moving story. The man's son had died about six months earlier, and he was trying to get his son's financial affairs in order. The son had several credit cards, including one from USAA with a $5,000 balance. When the father called USAA to discuss the debt, the representative interrupted him to ask how he and his wife were doing. Could she send the couple some materials on grieving? The gentleman said, "While other financial institutions [were] sending us delinquency notices and letters from attorneys, USAA's first response was to deal with our loss."

The representative on the phone was a member of USAA's Survivor Relations Team (SRT). The company receives notice of approximately 130 deaths of members each day; more than 26,000 USAA members die annually. Two and a half years ago, USAA organized the SRT to help members' families cope with the overwhelming business issues they face. Bryan Thomas, director of special services at USAA, told us, "We're reaching out to a member's family at a very difficult time. What positions us to be helpful is that we see our members as extensions of our family. So, quite naturally, when you experience a loss, you expect other family members to show love, care, and concern. It is as simple as a call to check on you and see how you are doing."

Losing a loved one is enough of a trauma, but there are also a host of administrative issues that must be dealt with: Credit-card accounts, billing statements, vehicle registrations, investments, insurance policies, and taxes are just a few. Everyone copes with these issues in unique ways; when it comes to grieving, no "one size fits all" approach is appropriate. Members of the SRT have been specifically trained in grief counseling, and all team members are skilled at intervening at any point in the grieving process, if the family so wishes. These savvy representatives don't attempt to inappropriately assert themselves as psychotherapists. The role of this unique group is to provide bereaved USAA members with expertise in understanding the business and financial aspects of death—and to do so when it is most critically needed.

When the company originally conceived of this program, USAA thought that the SRT's staff members would rotate; it assumed that its representatives would require a break from the intensity of the work and the emotional pain they encounter with survivors. But that has not been the case—every member of the original SRT has asked to continue. "By their own account, this has been the most rewarding job they've had, simply because it gives back," Bryan

What positions us to **be helpful** is that we **see our members** as extensions of **our family**.

Thomas explained. In the survivor–representative relationship, giving is reciprocal. Energized by the survivor's appreciation, the SRT member feels gratified and valued. One widow described her experience this way: "I was never involved in making investment decisions while married. I now have a complete understanding of each investment that I own and feel I am finally in control of my financial future."

In fact, USAA's educational foundation publishes the LifeGuide Series designed to walk members through each step of managing financial and administrative matters after a loss. In addition, the company provides a series of booklets, written by experts, on coping with loneliness, physical health, and helping your children grieve.

Do What's Right. The Money Will Follow

Parents often feel that equipping their children to become responsible adults is an act of love. But it's not an easy task in this highly

An example of the kind of communication USAA creates for the benefit of its young members.

commercialized, consumer-driven world. The question becomes, "How do you teach children to become reliable adults who know how to handle money wisely?" USAA helps this process by partnering with parents to offer advice and programs to help kids understand what it means to be responsible consumers.

In a publication titled "Under 25," young adults learn about renters' insurance, credit-card solicitors, buying a first car, and making the payments. USAA wants young people to be sophisticated customers when they walk into an auto dealership, and informed users of credit when they need it.

The company recently started a teen debit card that parents can preload up to a specific amount. Then the parents can follow online, in real time, where their child spends the money. Limits can be increased or decreased appropriately in order to facilitate the teenager's learning process, and money can be added instantly to cover emergencies.

"We make a **substantial investment** in **doing what's right,** knowing that it's going to be **profitable** eventually."

A few years ago, a major consulting firm advised USAA not to market investments to its members' children and, instead, to begin to expand their services for those in the 40-to-45 age group. But as Karen Presley, executive vice president of marketing, explained, such advice was off the mark, because the company's aim is first and foremost to help their members and their members' families manage their financial lives. Though it is a clever growth strategy, it requires patience, since the payoff is in the distant future. Presley explained, "We see it as having the opportunity to [influence] our future generations to be financially responsible, and you have to start out with them early." Bob Davis put it differently: "Is there a return on investment? Yes. What is that return? Who knows? But it's something we should do."

Though USAA's strategies would probably not work outside a military niche, its unique relationship with its members pays off. Compared with companies that serve the general public, USAA's delinquent fees and bankruptcies are virtually nonexistent. As Karen Presley told us, "We develop our marketing plan based on what our members need. We make a substantial investment in doing what's right, knowing that it's going to be profitable eventually."

Love on USS *Benfold*

Too many traditional managers put themselves above the people they lead. They view their own lives and jobs in color, yet they see the lives and jobs of those who work for them in black and white. Gutsy leaders recognize that everyone lives in color. They instinctively tear down the barriers separating management from those under them. With the empathy and insight to see beyond job descriptions, they are able to appreciate employees' entire lives, not just their time at the workplace. These leaders lead with love, which means making things easier for everyone.

One of the gutsy leaders we interviewed sets the standard for caring about his people and subordinating his needs to theirs. Michael Abrashoff is the former captain of USS *Benfold*, a $1-billion combat-missile destroyer. He turned a ship suffering from low morale, a weak reenlistment rate, and an overall poor performance into one of the best ships in the entire U.S. Navy. Reenlistment rates reached 100 percent, and morale soared. Abrashoff did it by devoting himself to his crew's needs, making his own secondary.

When we met Abrashoff in San Diego, he recounted the experience that changed his entire approach to leadership. As *Benfold*'s incoming skipper, Abrashoff attended the change-of-command ceremony at which his predecessor stepped down. At that event, Abrashoff witnessed something unprecedented. The whole crew of the ship, 310 men and women, stood on *Benfold*'s deck, literally cheering the departure of the outgoing commander. (Not a good thing.) The astounded Abrashoff knew instantly that many of the traditional command-and-control strategies he might have used to get his ship in shape weren't going to work. Instead, he went with his gut.

Early on, he realized that most of the young men and women under his command came from low-income families whose educa-

One of the Navy's most technologically advanced weapons: the USS *Benfold*, a $1-billion guided-missile destroyer.

tions were limited. For them, the Navy was a way out and up. Feeling a profound responsibility to help each proud, determined, young sailor, Abrashoff told us: "I consider it my job to improve my little 300-person piece of society, and that is as much a part of the bottom line as combat readiness." How big is your piece of society? Is it thirty people? Three hundred people? Is it more?

Love Is Listening

Abrashoff's first step, a novelty aboard *Benfold*, was to learn the names of all 310 crew members. But that, he quickly realized, wasn't enough. At two o'clock one morning, he woke up with an epiphany: "The only way I can create the right culture on this ship is to talk to every sailor in person, to communicate my goals, discover his or her goals, and build a bridge between the two."

Abrashoff immediately began one-on-one interviews. Before long, he was talking to five sailors every day. As he listened and learned, he changed as a leader. In fact, this commanding officer credits his crew with giving him far more than he gave them. His humility, interest, openness, and love are just a few of the reasons why Abrashoff's leadership of *Benfold* was so successful.

The interviews began with basics: hometown, family, ambitions, reason for enlisting. Abrashoff wanted to make personal connections with all crew members, which he hoped would help them relax and get a sense of him as someone who cared about them. Then he asked three specific questions about their views on *Benfold:* What did they like most about the ship? Least? What would they change if they could?

Three questions worth asking your people:

1. What do you like most about working here?
2. What do you like least about working here?
3. What would you change if you were in charge?

GUTS!

He wanted them to understand that his mission and their dreams were linked, "so they would see my goal of improving *Benfold* as an opportunity for them to apply their talents and give their jobs and their lives a real purpose."

Through the interviews, he developed enormous respect, indeed love, for his crew. "My sailors weren't born with anything remotely resembling a silver spoon in their mouths," he recounted. "But each and every one of them was trying to make something meaningful of their lives—they wanted to believe that what they were doing was important."

Abrashoff was consistent, and when the members of the crew came to believe that he was sincere, they confided their dreams, goals, and ideas for improving the ship. When he heard a good suggestion, he punched the public-address button and told everyone about it right away. "The turnaround time for launching a good idea was about five minutes," he recalled with a laugh.

The payoff was huge for Abrashoff, his crew, *Benfold*, and, ultimately, for the Navy:

- The cuisine improved markedly when 5 of its 13 cooks attended culinary school. Abrashoff financed their studies by buying provisions on the private market instead of from the Navy, enabling him to get higher-quality food for less money.
- Chores that failed to add value were eliminated. For example, one of Abrashoff's crew members realized that a new painting-and-coating process could preserve the ship's paint for 25 years; another suggested that all steel fastenings be replaced with stainless-steel alternatives. Together, these moves eliminated rust-chipping, the bane of every sailor's existence, as well as the need to paint the entire ship twice a year.

- Because of these and other initiatives, the ship was able to return $600,000 of its $2.5-million maintenance budget and $800,000 of its $3-million repair budget to the U.S. Navy's coffers.

By loving his sailors enough to trust their ideas, Abrashoff earned their love and created a reciprocity that enabled all hands to sharpen their skills and accelerate *Benfold*'s combat readiness. It became what Abrashoff wanted it to be—"the best damn ship in the Navy."

Believe in People

When someone you respect has confidence in you, you feel like a bigger, stronger, more capable person. When this happens at an organizational level, employees identify with the image their leader has of them and perform accordingly. Nothing proved *Benfold*'s progress more conclusively than the ship's first annual inspection under Abrashoff's command.

Once a year, outside inspectors visit all Navy ships to assess their combat readiness. Each ship and its crew are rated in 24 categories, with grades from basic (level one) to outstanding (level four). However, the system had a catch-22. Though the inspection's outcome was supposed to evaluate what further training the ship required to prepare it for combat, every ship, regardless of its inspection scores, trained for another six weeks.

Consistent with his character, Abrashoff saw this as an opportunity. He resolved that *Benfold* would steal a march on its sister ships and achieve level three. His ship would not be satisfied with a mediocre score. Since there weren't enough experienced officers to operate the ship and simultaneously prepare for inspection in all 24 categories, Abrashoff ordered the unthinkable: Junior petty officers would supervise the training in some of the categories. When his officers protested that this was unprecedented, Abrashoff said there

GUTS!

was no harm in trying and that the alternative was to do nothing and earn lower scores. The petty officers rallied to the cause. Proud to be chosen and determined to live up to the responsibility, their results in some areas eclipsed those of the senior officers.

In the crucial search-and-seizure exercise, aimed at foiling oil smugglers in the Persian Gulf, the inspectors balked at certifying work supervised by petty officers. But when Abrashoff insisted, they grudgingly assented and rated *Benfold* at level four. Across the board, the ship hit Abrashoff's target of level three.

Mike Abrashoff **proved** that **love** can **pay off**.

Shortly afterward, the Navy revised the assessment process. From that time on, if a ship could match *Benfold*'s performance, it was allowed to skip the next six weeks of training. Many did, and even more important, many more tried, which guaranteed that their crews would be better trained. Mike Abrashoff proved that love can pay off. He had the guts to listen to and learn from his people, and, as a result, he helped them succeed even in an organization as rigid as the U.S. Navy. Imagine what an equivalent act of love could do for your company.

Pass the Test of Time

From the beginning, Abrashoff's approach met with substantial opposition aboard his ship. "The greatest resistance to my interviews came from my mid-level managers," he recalled. "After all, most mid-level managers fear change and think primarily about their own job comfort. But once they realized that I wasn't interested in playing the blame game, but was just getting to know my people and get their suggestions for improving the ship, something amazing happened—

these middle managers found that their jobs became easier. They no longer had to spend hours a day micromanaging people, because the crew started taking initiative . . . instead of having to be told what to do. My mid-level people were suddenly freed up from a lot of their mundane responsibilities and had time to think long-range, to talk to other departments about ways to build shipwide unity."

"The **greatest resistance** to my interviews came from my **mid-level managers**."

When Abrashoff left *Benfold*, there wasn't a dry eye on the ship. What about your ship, your piece of society? Do the people you work with feel like you care about them enough to actively listen to their ideas and try them out?

A Bank Grounded in Love

Synovus, the financial-services giant, is an enterprise that was built on love more than 100 years ago.

One chilly morning during the winter of 1886, a young woman was working at the Eagle & Phenix cotton mill in Columbus, Georgia. She was conscientious and focused, saving every spare penny to build a better life for herself. Suddenly, her long skirt got caught in a piece of machinery, tearing it. Money spilled out across the wooden floor—the young woman had sewn all her savings into the hem of her skirt. Crying and frantic, she tried to gather the scattered bills and coins that represented her hopes for the future. But when she recovered it, the question was, what would she do next? She had no safe place to store her dreams. The local banks weren't interested in her meager business.

The secretary and treasurer of the mill, G. Gunby Jordan, was a practical businessman who genuinely cared about the welfare of his employees. When he heard about the incident, he was determined to find a solution. He felt that if people, like the young woman, were devoting themselves to the company, they were owed respect

Most employees want to do a good job. How they perform is simply a matter of whom they work for.

—DARRYL HARTLEY LEONARD

and compassion, as well as their paychecks. He suggested keeping her savings in the office safe. And he added a gutsy caveat: He proposed paying her interest every month. She accepted his offer and was amazed to see how her interest compounded. Before long, Jordan was tending to the savings of most of the mill's workers, which led to his opening a bank that has evolved into Synovus.

All through the years since, even as the company has expanded into every variety of sophisticated financial service and become a national leader in a whole other field, payment processing, it has remained true to its do-the-right-thing, small-town origins.

On the financial-services side, the company, which is listed on the New York Stock Exchange, owns 40 banks in small-town Alabama, Florida, Georgia, South Carolina, and Tennessee. As noted in Chapter 1, the Synovus family also includes Synovus Trust Company, among the Southeast's largest providers of trust services; Synovus Insurance, a provider of a full line of insurance products; Synovus Securities, a full-service brokerage firm; and Synovus Mortgage, which offers mortgage services across the Southeast.

Long before a decentralized management structure became the fad among consultants, Synovus's predecessor, Columbus Bank & Trust, was giving its individual banks the freedom to tailor their services to the varying needs of their individual customers. At the same time, the company has pioneered new techniques and technologies to improve and expand those services. It was one of the first to offer customers a revolving credit card, and, in recent years, it has developed a comprehensive asset-management unit to help customers build and preserve their wealth. Essentially, Synovus is leveraging the long-standing relationships its banks have with their customers to provide them with services ranging from insurance to private banking to corporate finance.

Synovus's credit-card expertise was capitalized on in 1974 when a division called TSYS (Total Systems Services) began moving electronic transactions for other credit-card banks, by telephone to begin with, then by satellite, and now by fiber-optic cables. Nine years later, TSYS was spun off as a separate, publicly traded enterprise to provide electronic-payments services. Synovus holds 81.1 percent of its shares, and it accounts for about a third of Synovus's overall revenue.

TSYS is a close second among payment processors to First Data of Denver, Colorado. In fact, as you read this, it may temporarily be in the lead because of a spring 2003 contract with Bank One. TSYS agreed to convert Bank One's 50 million credit-card accounts to its processing platform, TS2, by the summer of 2004, at which point TSYS will take over the processing task for two years.

"We could **be flexible** and **find a way** to **work with them,** or not play. We decided to be very flexible."

Why only two years? Because Bank One was determined to do the job itself, under a licensing agreement with TSYS, and do it sooner rather than later. It took Troy Woods, a TSYS executive vice president, almost a year to negotiate the deal. "We could be flexible and find a way to work with them, or not play," he said. "We decided to be very flexible."

Flexibility is also built into TS2, the most advanced processing system in the industry. It can support a variety of languages and currencies on a single platform—a major advantage for companies in international markets. The company also has an integrated payments platform for debit-card issuers and electronic benefit-transfer programs.

But banking is where it all started—and where the cultural core of the company remains.

A Culture of the Heart

When Bill Turner was eight years old, his grandfather, W. C. Bradley, took him aside for a little talk. That was when the young lad learned that he would someday control the family business, which included Columbus Bank & Trust as well as the W. C. Bradley Company. A local industrialist, Bradley had bought a major stake in the bank a few years after it was established by G. Gunby Jordan.

His grandfather's news was "a pretty heavy load," Turner said, but it gave him "years to observe my grandfather and my dad at work. The bad news was they didn't seem to do anything except walk around and listen to other people tell them what to do."

The concept of servant leadership was still in the future—it would be developed in the 1970s by AT&T executive and author Robert Greenleaf—but it was already alive and well in Columbus, and over time Bill Turner would come to personify that ideal. His journey was pungently punctuated by experiences that taught him the power of leading with love.

When Turner went to college, he learned how to run a business the "right way." He joined W. C. Bradley in 1947, starting as a director, and in due course he took the helm of the company, famous for making charbroil grills and accessories as well as other leisure products. He quickly set out to show his family what he had learned: "How to run a company in a traditional manner, where the boss is at the top of the pyramid. . . . It's the boss who shares his vision with the people. Of course, my vision was to create shareholder value, and that's not a bad vision, but it's just not big enough. The problem . . . is that everybody is trying to please the boss, not the customer. But probably the worst thing about an organization like that is [that] . . . trying to please the boss . . . make[s] him feel that he's omnipotent. . . . That kind of organization is lonely . . . slow . . . inflexible, and it's not very much fun."

"Then the Light Came On"

By conventional standards, Turner and his business were thriving, but, he said, "At age 32, I hit the wall. I had a wonderful wife, a lovely family, a beautiful home. I had gotten all the plaques that I'd ever need . . . but I was totally empty and exhausted and saying, 'Is this all there is to life?'"

At about this time, Turner was invited to a leadership seminar in Miami, Florida, where he heard a remark "that really changed my life. Someone said the antidote to exhaustion isn't necessarily rest. The antidote to exhaustion can be wholeheartedness. So I came back trying to figure out a way to . . . be wholehearted about what I was doing."

Turner had one epiphany after another. First, he realized that what was missing from his life was the sense that his work was worth doing; he felt no attachment to a community, nor any personal, intellectual, or spiritual growth. Then he understood that if he was unfulfilled in these areas, so were the people who worked for him. He defined a new goal—to create a common vision that offered everyone the chance to work together toward a better, more fulfilling life for all.

"The antidote to exhaustion can be wholeheartedness."

Turner realized that in order to bring this about, he had to understand the specific challenges his people faced. This meant listening to them, and responding to both their articulated and unspoken feelings. In essence, he needed to become a servant to them. "Then the light came on, and I said, 'That's what my grandfather and my dad had been doing.'"

At that point, Turner knew he was the guardian of an important family legacy. As he began talking with and getting to know his employees, he learned that "it wasn't enough to just meet the needs of people on the job. You have to love them and be concerned about their whole lives."

Focused on serving his people, Turner structured his day around making sure that everyone at the W. C. Bradley Company and at Synovus was provided with what he or she needed to be optimally productive at work and content at home. Obviously, there are limits to servant leadership, but Turner was determined to be a friend, mentor, and servant to his people to the fullest extent possible.

Describing his experience, Turner said: "I've learned that . . . when you push power away, you have more . . . because it empowers everyone else. I've learned that there's no limit to what you can do if you don't care who gets the credit for it. . . . I've learned that a negative will kill the positive in any situation—in business, in the com-

> The key to your impact as a leader is your own sincerity. Before you can inspire with emotion, you must be swamped with it yourself. Before you can move their tears, your own must flow. To convince them, you must yourself believe.
>
> **—WINSTON CHURCHILL**

"I've learned that there's **no limit** to **what you can do** if you don't care **who gets the credit** for it."

munity, in the family, in the home . . . I've learned that there is a tremendous energy and creativity in people if you just get out of the way . . . encourage them, and be their cheerleader. And more

At Synovus, customer care is not a program; it is a covenant.

important, I've learned that servant leadership attracts people who want to be servant leaders, and it transforms [them] . . . into servant leaders. . . . I'm Exhibit A right here."

Be Passionate

Bill Turner was named chairman of the board in 1982, and he now serves as chairman of the executive committee. During most of his years with the company, two men named James Blanchard, father and then son, have been chief executive. We were eager to hear Synovus's current CEO talk about servant leadership, and he didn't disappoint. In the words of Blanchard the son, "People who commit to work for us have given us one of the most valuable things they have—their working energy. In return, the company should serve their interests at least as well as they serve the company. You have to have a passion for making your company a great place to work. . . . And you have to develop a leadership cadre that practices servant leadership."

Synovus managers share that vision. When Blair Carnahan graduated from the Wharton School of Business, he was hired to work on a Synovus Internet project headed by Lisa White. Carnahan considers her the model of a servant leader. In his view, White's full-time job was "to make sure that we were a well-oiled machine, that we were all happy, not only in the job but in our lives, which is something that most bosses don't really concern themselves with." Early in the project, Carnahan's wife received a handwritten note from White along with a gift certificate, acknowledging the demands that Synovus was asking of her husband. Carnahan said that "Lisa opened up her home to us, her heart to us. What more could you ask from a boss?"

All Synovus employees are treated equally. Carla Jean Renzello of Valparaiso, Florida, recalled her first taste of servant leadership: "In 1996, after . . . working for Vanguard Bank [a Synovus bank] as a part-time teller for only 18 months, my daughter suffered a collapsed lung. She was hospitalized three times in a three-month period and endured six operations. Through all of this, I learned the true meaning of Synovus's 'culture of the heart.' My branch manager and all of the management of Vanguard Bank were partners with me in her care. Dinner was brought to my other daughter at our home because I spent nights at the hospital. Today, my little girl is healthy, and I am the head teller at our branch and very proud to be a member of the Synovus family."

In love-centered organizations like Synovus, people respond to being cared for with loyalty, trust, and stronger performances. The

> Where love rules, there is no will to power, and where power predominates, love is lacking. The one is the shadow of the other.
>
> —CARL JUNG

measure of their fidelity is that their excellent training and experience make them prime targets for recruiters from other organizations, but they don't leave. As Jim Blanchard pointed out: "We record the history of a company by tracking its profits and revenues, mergers and acquisitions, contracts and losses. But it is the countless little moments every day that make a company great week by week: Birthday cakes, handshakes, hallway chats, and shared memories become the shared vision."

A Special Sanctuary

Frederic Holzberger, founder, president, and chief executive of Fredric's, is a gutsy leader who openly expresses his love for the company's exclusive line of Aveda beauty products. And he certainly expresses his loving feelings for his employees who share his environmental concerns. In 2001, Holzberger staged his tenth annual Aveda/Fredric's Mid-America tour at the Cincinnati Convention Center. For more than 2,300 guests, the host dished up not only his usual lavish menu of edible delights and stirring speeches, but also stress-relieving massages for hundreds of feet, hands, and scalps.

Salon owners arriving from all four corners of Fredric's distribution empire were salved and soothed at an "Evening Garden" networking event, in an "Experience Shrine," featuring plush sofas, massage chairs, seven Chakra sculptures, and a candlelit waterfall. "We take care of people, and they, in turn, will take care of the industry and the future," said Holzberger. Speakers flown in from around the world shared their expertise on skin care, makeup, and hair care.

Before he was involved with Aveda/Fredric's, Holzberger held many low-paying jobs, including hauling garbage, delivering newspapers, and chopping onions for Coney Dogs. "My family had to work very hard just to survive. And after seeing how employers treated me and other people along the way, I set some personal benchmarks:

- "I will never ask an employee to do something I wouldn't do myself."
- "People don't join a company; they buy into it."
- "If you create an environment that is friendly to your number-one customers, your employees, and your business partners, [they] . . . will . . . want to come to work."
- "If you take care of your employees, they will take care of your customers."

A notably idealistic enterprise, suffused with Holzberger's environmentalism, Fredric's is headquartered on six pristine acres in the midst of an industrial row in Fairfield, Ohio.

Fredric's has the feel of a sanctuary. Local and visiting employees benefit from the on-site Child Nurturing Center; the organic Brown House Café; and the 2,000-square-foot greenhouse, which is designed to grow herbs, plants used for skin care, and organic

"We **take care of people**, and they, in turn, will **take care of the industry** and the **future**."

fruits and vegetables. But don't be fooled by the environment's beauty: A lot of work gets done here. "Business isn't just about making your quarter," Holzberger said. "It's about going deeper and deeper with people, with your customers, and with your environment. It's not for everyone, and it's not to say we are better than anyone else. It's just to say we are different." This difference is paying off. Fredric's finished 2002 with more than $36 million in revenues and a growth rate of 13 percent.

Not long ago, Holzberger received the Creative Thinking Association's national award for "excellence and superior creative achievement," presented for his creativeness in caring for others. In 1994, he founded Project Daymaker, a nonprofit organization that brings beauty services to those in need. Holzberger purchased and transformed a 34-foot Winnebago into a salon on wheels. The vision behind the project was for licensed professionals to donate their time and expertise to those less fortunate. Project Daymaker has now helped people all across the country, from New York to Los Angeles, as well as its home-based territory of Ohio, Michigan, Indiana, and Kentucky. Targeting homeless shelters and treatment centers for adults and children, it offers a great opportunity for salon professionals to get involved and give back to their communities.

Holzberger's inspiration came from his relationship with Sister Bonnie Steinlage of the Franciscan Sisters for the Poor in Hamilton, Ohio, a friend and spiritual adviser who has a similar (though stationary) program called St. John Project Daymaker. Sister Bonnie had spent 22 years as a nursing nun, and it was taking its toll on her. Then one day her ministry took a turn. It happened while she was fasting and praying in a little hospital chapel. She was both taken aback and stirred by a verse from the Gospel according to Matthew: "When you fast and pray, wash your face and comb your hair." This verse was her sign to become a licensed cosmetologist. As a start, she set up shop in a tiny little bathroom at a homeless shelter in one of Cincinnati's poorest and most dangerous neighborhoods. Sister Bonnie's sense of compassion is contagious, and her place in life is beyond mere coincidence.

We spent an unforgettable evening with her at one of Frederic Holzberger's events. She laughed with us as she remembered growing up in a poor home and how she hated having to run outside in the bitter cold to use the family outhouse. She told us, "It's all really a blessing. I had always wished for my own bathroom!"

It was in 1992 that Frederic Holzberger first met Sister Bonnie at an educational hair event. And it was at that event that he first heard of Sister Bonnie's inspired vision to cut hair for the poor and homeless on a full-time basis. Holzberger was so moved by her compassion and dream that he immediately donated Aveda products to all of the beauty-care centers associated with Sister Bonnie. The success of that connection further inspired Holzberger to create a salon on wheels to provide beauty-care services and personal-hygiene education to those

"Has **love** been the **driving force** in all my activities **today**?"

in need. He hoped to build self-esteem and self-responsibility in the people they touch. Aveda salon volunteers donate their time and services to Project Daymaker, hoping to ultimately assist these individuals back into the workforce. Since its inception, the 34-foot roaming Salon has traveled more than 80,000 miles and Project Daymaker has served and touched more than 6,000 people with the help of more than 1,500 licensed salon volunteers.

When Aveda requested a list of all the charities and organizations that Holzberger supports, it was four pages long. At that point, Aveda recognized Holzberger for his community leadership, noting that the company is a "salon brand, a service brand, and a loving brand. A loving touch is the key to our success!"

Love's Bottom Line

Though businesses around the world spend billions training people to become better leaders, no course teaches them how to love. How could we overlook a competence so essential to leadership?

The gutsy leaders we've met aren't afraid to ask themselves, "Has love been the driving force in all my activities today? Did I express it in my conversations with the board, a customer, or a supplier?" In our view, what matters isn't how others have treated you; it's how you have treated others despite their treatment of you. It takes true leadership and real guts to love people when they aren't lovable.

For gutsy leaders, this is the key commandment: Do unto others what enables them to succeed, regardless of what they do unto you. And what's in it for you? In business as in life, the bottom line is that love trumps money. We had General Cooney, the former deputy chief executive officer of USAA, in a leadership program we hosted a few years ago at Southwest Airlines. At the end of the program, we asked participants what they had gotten out of the retreat. Cooney, a man who defines the term gutsy leader, said: "One of the last things

Do unto others what **enables** them **to succeed, regardless** of what they do unto you.

I have to accomplish before retiring is to revamp our leadership-training program. I am going back, and I'm going to see to it that we teach the future leaders of USAA how to LOVE." Now, that comes from a highly decorated military officer who helped build a $66 billion financial-services company. Recently, we met with Cooney again, and this time he said, "The litmus test for every decision must be, 'Will it earn the respect, love, and admiration of family and friends?' Because at the end of the journey that is all that really matters!" If only more leaders had such guts and a readiness to show, not tell, how to love more, what a better world we would live in.

✓ **Check your assumptions about love:** Do you understand the crucial role of love in your business? For the gutsy leaders we've met, love is a choice as well as an emotion. It has less to do with how you feel and more to do with how you behave.

✓ **Choose service over self-interest:** Love is most often expressed through service. For example, those of us with children will cart them back and forth between their activities, even when doing so is inconvenient and exhausting. We serve them because we love them. When USAA chose to accept late premium payments for the life-insurance policies of two deceased members, it chose service over self-interest. What motivated your major decisions over the last few months—service or self-interest?

✓ **Care about the person behind the customer:** How well do you know the individuals who are your customers? Are they more than a market segment to you? They must be if you want to serve them well. Follow USAA's Bob Davis's lead. Hold monthly meetings in which you present to your employees profiles of your customers to bring the former into the lives of the latter. Design the profiles to motivate and inspire employees to feel empathic toward their customers' unique concerns. Customers will respond with loyalty and dedication to those who are genuinely interested in the challenges they face.

✓ Care about the person behind the employee:

Get to know your people in as much depth as possible, which means being interested in their lives away from work. The more you can help your people seamlessly bridge their work and home lives, the better your organization will perform.

Toward this end, begin to understand each person as a distinct individual with unique problems and passions. Find out what people want and need. Often, the concern is child care. If you can empathize with that worry, you could probably mitigate anxiety by helping people integrate their children into their work lives. If so, your employees, energized by their relief, will have more of themselves to give to their jobs.

✓ Make trust the foundation of your professional relationships:

In general, the degree of trust in a relationship determines its quality. Without it, we chronically feel suspicious, unsafe, and insecure. In a work environment that lacks trust, a spirit of commitment and cooperation will find neither fertile ground nor nourishment to grow. Trusting others is what allows people to take risks, collaborate, and unite behind a cause.

One way to ensure that trust prevails in your organization is to create a cultural trust committee. For more than a century, trust has been the main ingredient in Synovus's relationships with its employees and customers. In fact, it has an interdepartmental Cultural Trust Committee that meets with the CEO monthly to discuss and develop ways of keeping the enterprise's core commitment relevant and vital.

✓ Make trust a performance measure:

TD Industries, the Texas-based mechanical and electrical contractor, is another company that overtly states the importance of trust. In fact, it is a key measure of a manager's performance, which means that all managers are urged to maintain a "trust balance sheet" with every employee on their teams.

✓ Show people how to build and break trust:

TDI provides its managers with a list of behaviors guaranteed to either promote trust or guarantee that it will never occur. Although they are obvious, a few bear repeating. Among the trust breakers are: Treat your people discourteously; ridicule them behind their backs; play favorites; never admit a mistake; break promises. The trust builders include: Offer understanding and support in times of stress; give people a chance to talk while you actively listen; care about each person's family, interests outside of work, and values. And the most important one is: Trust your people.

As Jack Lowe Jr., chairman and chief executive of TDI, said: "Building trust is a journey, not a destination." Trust doesn't just happen; it's something you have to protect and promote every day. Could your organization benefit from a trust committee or by keeping trust balance sheets?

✓ Help others become successful: Synovus's fundamental belief that every individual has worth motivates it to help each employee reach her or his full potential. Its leaders are expected to create opportunities that will advance their team members, facilitate their individual growth, and coach them toward optimum performance. This means that leaders are accessible to their teams, are willing to serve them, and are invested in their ongoing success. Several specific programs (branded by the theme "treat folks right and do the right thing") reinforce this objective:

- **Right from the Start.** In an effort to make sure things are "Right from the Start," Synovus has designed a program to teach its newest team members about the company's "Culture of the Heart." New people are welcomed into the Synovus family and helped to understand the company's philosophy. Intending to make people feel special as soon as they arrive, the process demonstrates Synovus's commitment to their success.

- **Right Choice.** Under the banner "Right Choice," Synovus employees are taught how to maximize their benefits. Concerned about the financial well-being of its people, the company inspires them to take advantage of its wealth-building plan. Employees who hit specified targets can earn up to 21 percent of their annual gross salaries in bonuses.

  Through its "Family Education Leave," Synovus offers 20 hours of paid time off for employees to spend with their children—in a classroom, on a field trip, or in whatever way they choose. Considering itself a family, Synovus, like USAA, proves its respect for employees by helping them integrate their work and personal lives—an especially challenging task for parents.

- **Right Steps.** Synovus recognizes that people change; their goals, skills, dreams, and worries all evolve in one way or another. In response, it designed a program called Right Steps to help "Individual Performance Development." In Right Steps, team leaders and members discuss their changing needs and desires, then work together on developing strategies to meet them. While some people want to advance, others seek a lateral move into a new area, and still others want to change their status from full- to part-time. Together, team leaders and members bring these changes about. Stronger trust and bolstered performances are the results.

- **Personally Developing EveryONE.** PDE, as it is known at Synovus, is a multifaceted initiative that includes the "Leadership Institute," the

MAKING THE RIGHT CHOICE

ADOPTION ASSISTANCE • TUITION ASSISTANCE • FAMILY EDUCATION LEAVE
REACH VOLUNTEER • MEDICAL PLAN • STOCK PURCHASE PLAN

For your time, your health, your wealth and your well-being

Caring for each individual and helping balance these areas of life is the right thing to do. It makes life that much easier - which can only make life at work that much better.

R I G H T

C H O I C E

CE. YOU MAKE IT RIGHT.

A communication piece promoting the Synovus Right Choice Program.

"Cultural Trust Committee," "Foundations of Leadership," and other programs that fall under the "Right Choice" brand. The ultimate goal is to ensure that all employees are offered opportunities to develop to their fullest potential.

Synovus CEO Jim Blanchard explains PDE this way: "Personally Developing EveryONE to a higher power is our effort to strengthen where we live, starting with where we work. It's based on our company's most enduring value: Every person has great worth. If Synovus employees want to take college courses, the company will help them. If they want to get in better shape, the corporation has a fitness center, fitness classes, and offers discounted health-club memberships. If they want to move up to a position of more responsibility, training will be provided. If they are having difficulties on the job, the organization will find them a mentor." This focus on continuous improvement has helped build Synovus a workforce that is second to none in its commitment, performance, and morale.

Reinforcing Blanchard, Elizabeth R. James, Synovus's vice chairman and chief information officer, declared, "We believe in the worth of the individual and we're gonna make sure people are growing professionally, financially, personally, spiritually."

What's your next move? If you're committed to "treating folks right" and "doing the right thing," think about each of your team members and ask these questions: Have we done everything to make him or her successful? Have we given him or her the right opportunities to excel? Has he or she received substantive feedback? Have we helped every employee create an individual development plan?

✓ **Listen hard, act fast:** We believe that nothing expresses love better than listening to and hearing what people have to say. It is a primary way of expressing your concern and appreciation for another person and his or her ideas. Follow Captain Abrashoff's example and ask your employees these three questions: What do you love about working here? What do you hate? If you were in charge, what would you change? Then act on what you've learned.

✓ **Get rid of the obstacles:** At the end of the workday, people go home feeling either energetic or drained of all energy, depending on how many obstacles they encountered during the day. What causes the obstacles? What keeps your employees from moving with speed and agility? What makes it difficult for them to serve customers? What frustrates them? If the answers lie in your systems and structures, remake them so that they are simple and enabling, as opposed to complex and disabling. Doing so is an act of love. Blow up the barriers that hold your employees back. As we've said before, flatten the hierarchy, require fewer signatures, and promote informal communications. Develop a reputation for freeing smart people from dumb processes.

✓ **Feel it, don't fix it:** When people complain about their work, sometimes what they really want is to be understood. At Southwest Airlines, the Inflight Department, which is responsible for scheduling the captains and first officers, had been complaining for years about the difficulty of its duties at holiday time. Inevitably they're asked to process a flood of last-minute calls from colleagues requesting schedule changes.

After hearing the complaints, Kelleher finally said, "Okay, that's it! I'm there!" You can imagine that when the first few pilots called to rearrange their schedules and Kelleher answered the phone, the calls probably took an immediate new twist. But it isn't likely that he made huge changes to the schedules. Kelleher's presence was significant because it reflected his readiness to experience and share Inflight's troubles. Frequently, that's exactly what your people are asking for as well; they want you to understand and experience what it's like for them during their departments' most stressful times.

✓ Liberate people from the constraints of politics and fear: It's impossible to overstate the harm caused by political infighting. First, it wastes time and energy that should be invested in improving performance. Second, it divides your people. Third, it reflects and perpetuates fear and mistrust. Fourth, the climate it creates—"everyONE for him- or herself"—is the antithesis of love. There is no "I" in love. Gutsy leaders recognize this and try to stop it before it begins.

If you run an open organization with no hidden agendas, you're making it nearly impossible for rumors to gain steam. If merit, not politics, is the basis for all rewards and promotions, those who complain about the system will lose credibility. Let everyone at every level in your organization know that you will not tolerate petty politics, tribalism, and infighting. In its description of the importance of openness, Synovus's credo states: "In our halls, every person must know his or her value. Every individual must know his or her worth. We will create a workplace where our corporate family members feel safe, free from harassment, free from mistreatment, free from secrecy, free from petty manipulation." We suggest that your company take those words to heart.

✓ Take a chance on someone: Gutsy leaders demonstrate their faith in people. When Mike Abrashoff made a major inspection of his ship the responsibility of junior sailors, he put his career on the line, which communicated beyond a

doubt his belief in his crew. In response, his crew came through for him. Benefit from Captain Abrashoff's experience and do the same. Find or create projects that allow people to demonstrate their talent. Perhaps in your company it's taking the lead on a major conference call, making the pitch to a potential customer, or setting up an important meeting. However you do it, relinquish control and show your employees how much you believe in them.

✓ **Be patient with people:** Whether you are negotiating a contract, helping someone learn a new technology, or explaining the nuances of a complicated deal, being patient tops the list of characteristics that embody love. But being patient does not mean accepting mediocre performance or tolerating dysfunctional behavior. You'll know that's happening if your efforts bear no results. Having patience is a vital way of demonstrating how much we care about others.

✓ **Display your appreciation:** AFLAC devotes an entire week each year to show its employees how much it values them. In addition to award ceremonies, gifts, and a gala banquet, senior managers deliver personal thank-yous to their departments. Children are invited to come see where Mom or Dad works, and a pep rally featuring entertainers and motivational speakers follows. On Saturday, AFLAC treats all employees and their families to a day at Six Flags amusement park. Parents enjoy having their children watch as praise is heaped upon Mom or Dad.

Prepare a list of your team members and, on a sheet of paper, note two or three very specific things that each person has done that are worthy of affirmation. Then look for a natural opportunity, preferably in public, to share your observations.

✓ Show compassion to both your customers and employees:
USAA could fulfill its mandate simply by selling life insurance, but it does far more. Its Survivor Relations Team exemplifies the company's genuine empathy with its customers' anguish and its wish to relieve that pain. It is not surprising that members respond to this compassion with their trust.

Build a nonintrusive, informal network of people who will let you know if someone is having a particularly difficult time. Everyone at Southwest Airlines, for example, knows that the executive office wants to hear about someone enduring a crisis or serious problem. When Colleen Barrett sends a note or gift, the employee is genuinely touched.

✓ Show your vulnerability:
It takes more guts to express a wide range of emotions than it does to appear wooden and stoical. It can be difficult, if not impossible, to relate to a leader who knows everything, is unafraid, invulnerable, and always in control. Whether it is intentional or not, such behavior is intimidating and alienating.

Conventional thinking in business dismisses an expression of vulnerability as weak, even inappropriate. Yet if we look at the leaders people follow—human beings with whom they can identify—it is traditional thinking that should be dismissed. For example, in the wake of the events of September 11, 2001, New York's mayor, Rudolph Giuliani, became a national hero and *Time* magazine's Person of the Year. In our view, it was because Giuliani shared his emotions with the nation while, at the same time, he confidently took charge.

✓ Use tough love:
Leading with love means having the guts to tell people the truth; it means you can't avoid doing

so just because you don't want to cope with the hurt feelings you may evoke. You may, in fact, be helping them avoid greater, unnecessary pain later. Avoiding the truth allows the problem to fester—to the company's and the individual's detriment.

CHAPTER 6

Gutsy Leaders Make Business Heroic

In our personal lives, we recognize the need to be involved in social causes. We enroll in community groups, attend church or temple, contribute to blood drives, and read to the illiterate. All these acts show the basic human impulse to transcend our daily concerns and do good by connecting with something bigger than self-interest.

A leader who dismisses this need as irrelevant to his or her company is, in a sense, rejecting an aspect of people's humanity. The

P eople are capable of the highest generosity and self-sacrifice. But they have to feel and believe that what they are doing is truly heroic, timeless, and supremely meaningful. The crisis of modern society is precisely that people no longer feel heroic.

—ERNEST BECKER

rejection tells them to bring only certain parts of themselves to work every day—the part that wants a paycheck. Clueless managers depreciate the intellectual, physical, and emotional capital, which is crucial for building a company's competitiveness. A good business values its people above all its other resources. A bad business is invariably tone-deaf to the value of human capital.

Behind most great organizations is a moral imperative, an obligation or sense of duty that inspires people to act in certain ways. To an important degree, people are drawn to these enterprises because they want to be part of an organization that has a noble purpose, to feel they are participating in something meaningful.

Nowhere is this more evident than at Medtronic, the world's largest manufacturer of implantable biomedical devices, such as neurostimulators, heart valves, pacemakers, and defibrillators. The company's 28,000 employees are well aware that, every 12 seconds or so, someone's life is improved by a Medtronic product or therapy. It is a major reason they are so passionate about what they do.

Medtronic researchers and scientists worldwide have been awarded more than 3,000 patents. *The Economist* magazine describes Medtronic as "the most innovative and market-savvy firm in the $160-billion-a-year medical device industry." In fact, more than 70 percent of the company's $6 billion in annual revenues comes from products introduced just in the last two years. They have given Medtronic a compounded annual growth rate of 17 percent over the last decade.

Bill George, Medtronic's former chairman and chief executive officer, said, "I think our success can be directly traced to our passion for the Medtronic mission." Nearly 35 years ago, Earl Bakken, Medtronic's cofounder, drafted a statement that articulates the orga-

Medtronic's Head-
quarters, Minneapolis,
Minnesota.

nization's mission: "Alleviate pain, restore health, and extend life."
To help people embrace this cause, Bakken initiated a "medallion
ceremony." After six months, new employees receive bronze medals;
on one side is the company's corporate symbol—a human figure rising up out of bed—and on the other is the mission statement. The
message of the medallion ceremony is clear: "You're not here just to
make money for the company or yourself, but to help restore people
to full life and health."

Bakken's statement and the medallion unite Medtronic employees worldwide in a common cause. As Medtronic's current chief
executive, Arthur Collins Jr., noted, "It's a form of initiation ritual

A corporate symbol of Medtronic's mission: "to alleviate pain, restore health, and extend life."

and . . . [it's] an important part of our culture here. It transcends product lines, geography, race, and culture."

Medtronic's genesis is a case study in the strange and wonderful ways great companies come about. It was born of a conversation in the spring of 1949 between two friends, Earl Bakken and Palmer Hermundslie, in Minneapolis. Bakken was a graduate student in electrical engineering at the University of Minnesota, and Hermundslie worked for a lumber company. Bakken was explaining how he had gotten to know the people at Northwestern Hospital when he came by to pick up his wife, a medical technologist. Once staff members found out what Bakken was studying, they started asking him to repair delicate electronic equipment that was beyond the ability of the hospital's engineers.

During that fateful conversation, Bakken and Hermundslie agreed to go into business together, establishing a company that would specialize in the repair of medical equipment. Bakken dropped out of graduate school, and Hermundslie quit his job. Medtronic, as they called the business, had a slow start, but gradually became better known among doctors and nurses all through the

Midwest. Eventually, the organization began to sell other companies' medical products.

Once again, fate intervened. Research teams at the hospitals asked Medtronic to modify some of their lab equipment, and that led to requests that the company actually design and create new devices for specific tests. Suddenly, the two friends were in the manufacturing business, turning out dozens of one-shot products. Among their customers was Dr. C. Walton Lillehei, a University of Minnesota heart surgeon, who asked if Medtronic could develop a battery-powered pacemaker that could comfortably be worn externally. Bakken's design did the job, a major breakthrough in the treatment of cardiac problems. In 1960, after reading a paper by two New York physicians describing their research with a self-contained, long-term pacemaker, Hermundslie flew his small plane through a rainstorm to Buffalo to meet with the physicians; he left with their signatures on a contract giving Medtronic exclusive rights to manufacture and market their invention.

Having claimed the majority of the pacemaker market, the corporation proceeded to expand into every variety of medical device, mainly through a series of acquisitions. Today its products include spinal-implant devices, drug-delivery systems, catheters and stents, surgical tools, and devices for the treatment of diabetes and urological problems. The wide range of its products makes it possible for Medtronic to offer hospitals bundles of devices at competitive prices. By 2002, the company's market capitalization had reached $598 million.

Along with its products, Medtronic provides customers with in-person, hands-on technical service and support—a long-standing tradition that began with Earl Bakken rushing into operating rooms to solve electrical problems and Palmer Hermundslie flying his plane around the country to make emergency deliveries of pacemakers. Its customer support also takes the form of customer education, with Medtronic sponsoring all sorts of seminars, symposia, and workshops at which physicians and other health care specialists can learn how to use its equipment.

The quality of the company's customer service relies on the dedication, skill, and enthusiasm of its employees, and that's where the Medtronic mission comes in. The organization constantly nurtures their feelings of being part of a heroic cause. For example, each December for more than 39 years, Medtronic has invited six physicians and their patients to explain to employees how a Medtronic product has changed, or even saved, their lives. To an auditorium-packed audience of 1,500 and several thousand more watching via satellite, these are moving stories.

Bill George pointed out that every Medtronic employee has a "defining moment" when the cause evolves from an intellectual concept to a true passion. For George, that moment came at his first holiday program. There, he met T. J. Flack, an 18-year-old suffering from

Every Medtronic employee has a **"defining moment"** when the cause evolves **from an intellectual concept** to a **true passion**.

cerebral palsy since birth. He had lived with incredible pain and frustration for the first 17 years of his life. Flack had surgery every June, followed by months in a body cast, only to watch his spasms return throughout the year. When he was 16, he refused more surgery and his body became increasingly rigid. Then Medtronic came out with a programmable pump that can deliver medication to Flack's spinal cord. T. J.'s quality of life improved dramatically. His speech became better, he could get out of bed and get dressed by himself, and he was able to climb the steps to his school alone.

The drug-pump division at Medtronic had been failing for years, but George was so moved by Flack's story that, instead of selling off the failing drug-pump business as he had intended, he restructured it. More resources were devoted to research and development and marketing and sales. The pump business was restored to profitability and quickly became one of Medtronic's fastest-growing product lines. Moreover, the technology has become a platform from which new therapies have continued to emerge.

In its annual survey of the "best companies to work for" in the United States, *Fortune* magazine found that "86 percent of Medtronic employees said their work had special meaning; 94 percent felt pride in what they accomplished." One of those employees, Justine Fritz, a member of Medtronic's marketing group, leads a 12-member team that manages a multitude of products—among them

> For the secret of man's being is not only to live, but to have something to live for.
>
> —FYODOR DOSTOYEVSKY

brochures, manuals, sales manuals, and insurance forms—associated with a new product launch. In talking about the importance of her work, Fritz said: "I've . . . never worked on anything that so visibly, so dramatically changes the quality of somebody's life." Most recently, Fritz has been a key player in marketing Medtronic's Activa Parkinson's control therapy, which uses an implanted device to stimulate the nervous system electronically. The device is designed to reduce tremors and other symptoms of advanced Parkinson's disease.

People come to work **not only for a paycheck** but to **make a difference**.

We aren't surprised to see that employees at Medtronic like Fritz find special meaning in their work. Bill George related the following story from a medallion ceremony at Medtronic's European headquarters in Lausanne, Switzerland. A Swiss farmer suffering from

Parkinson's disease tremors demonstrated his symptoms to the audience by turning off his Medtronic neurostimulation device. The tremors returned immediately, offering a vivid demonstration to the audience of 150 new employees of the importance of their work. In that moment, manufacturing lifesaving devices became more than just a job.

People don't stay at Medtronic because they have on-site child-care, fitness centers, massages, and free dry cleaning. The same is true of employees at Quad/Graphics, SAS, and USAA. They are drawn to and remain at the company because the work is fulfilling.

Here is how Medtronic reinforces its heroic cause:

- Its cause is prominently displayed throughout its factories and offices.

- It has established a "wall of patients" in the company's executive area.

- Patient pictures and stories are featured in the annual report.

- Its cause is carved in stone at the base of a statue of founder Earl Bakken outside company headquarters.

- The chief executive holds monthly employee breakfasts to discuss whether the company is living up to its mission.

- He also sends regular e-mails to employees describing how Medtronic is actively pursuing its goals.

- Its cause is reflected in the recruiting process, the acquisition process, and in meetings with physicians and shareholders.

- Its cause becomes the template over which executives make decisions about benefits and profit-sharing plans.

- An annual survey is conducted to ensure that everyone in the company understands the Medtronic cause.

Medtronic puts so much energy into embedding its cause because the organization clearly understands that employees' lives have more meaning when their work has lasting significance.

It's More Than a Paycheck

We all want to believe in what we do. If you have held a job that conflicted with your value system or that, in your view, contributed little to the world, there is no way you would give your heart and soul to your work. It ensures mediocre performance and higher-than-average turnover. People come to work not only for a paycheck but to make a difference. Studies that ask employees to rank their priorities at work show that meaning-

> When you cease to make a contribution, you begin to die.
> **—ELEANOR ROOSEVELT**

ful work outranks compensation. We think that virtually everyone wants to be part of something that transcends his or her everyday life. When our hearts and minds are engaged, we feel inspired to use our gifts and talents generously to the benefit of others.

The gutsiest leader in history, Jesus, as well as other gutsy leaders such as Gandhi, Joan of Arc, Martin Luther King Jr., and Mother Teresa, to name a few, did not set out to become world-renowned leaders. They set out to pursue a cause so compelling and so powerful that others got caught up in the movement. Their passion to address a need and create a better world captivated people's hearts and minds, drawing them to make personal and professional sacrifices for the good of the cause. Gutsy leaders believe in their causes so deeply that their faith ignites the power and potential of those around them. Define your business in terms of a cause that makes the world a better place, and you will cut to the very heart of true motivation.

Several years ago, we led a seminar that was attended by a number of people from a Kodak photoprocessing center. We asked everyone in the room, "What's heroic about what you do?" We received a lot of answers: "We exceed our customers' expectations." "The clarity of our prints is unmatched." "Customers can count on the reliability and speed of our service."

Finally, a woman in the back of the room stood up and said, "That's all true, but it isn't heroic. Our work is heroic because we preserve people's memories—the birth of a child, a wedding, an exotic vacation. We capture some of the most important times of people's lives."

There was silence for a moment. Then a murmur of excitement coursed through the room. We could feel the level of energy and engagement rise. Why? Because that woman got it right. What ignites enthusiasm and inspires performance more? Saying that you process film and paper better than anyone else, or saying that you capture the moments that make life rich and interesting? Suddenly, these photo processors had a cause that put their work in a larger context, one that made a positive contribution to the world. What had been an advertising slogan was suddenly a reality in their lives, something that gave their work meaning and significance.

Southwest Airlines has the most motivated and productive workforce in the airline industry, because its employees understand their work to be more about freedom than about flying. In a letter to the employees of Southwest, Herb Kelleher clearly articulated the nature of their cause. Here is an excerpt:

> We have done something for over 25 years that no other airline has ever attempted and successfully achieved: We have democratized the skies. We have allowed people from every walk of life to go, see, and do things that they never thought possible. We have given our customers the freedom to fly. The Wright Brothers would be proud!
>
> So, in a real sense, we are not just in the airline business. We are in the freedom business.
>
> It is because of your commitment to serve our customers and each other with your magnificent sense of humor and humanity—and because of your relentless efforts to keep our costs lower than the competition—that we have been able to make air travel affordable and become a symbol of freedom to millions of Americans.
>
> You are my pride; my inspiration, and, truly, my symbol of freedom!

Connecting people's individual contributions to the larger cause comes naturally for Herb Kelleher. He believes that the people of Southwest Airlines deliver a product that has tremendous social value. By exercising the discipline to stay focused on its core competence, Southwest has helped consumers save billions of dollars in airfare. When Southwest enters a market, it usually offers fares 30

When the business becomes a crusade, what follows is a movement.

to 50 percent below those of its competitors. This means the child of divorced parents can see Mom or Dad more often, the elderly widow on a limited income can visit family and friends, and the entrepreneur in Phoenix can woo potential customers in Albuquerque, Tucson, El Paso, and Salt Lake City.

The mantra at Southwest Airlines is: It's not a job, it's a crusade. Ron Ricks, Southwest's senior vice president of governmental affairs, explained: "The principle—the higher calling, if you will—that drives Southwest employees is 'How can we protect the people who fly our airline? How can we protect small businesses? Are we doing what's best for senior citizens who count on us for low fares?'"

Though this hasn't been officially studied, ramp agents estimate that one out of every eight little Disney or Sesame Street suitcases they place on the belt loader belongs to a child whose parents are separated. Whether that is statistically true or not, it is an idea that motivates Southwest to turn those airplanes on time. Southwest has done a magnificent job of helping its ramp agents see how the mundane, isolated events of the everyday can have a huge impact on the business of freedom.

When the business becomes a crusade, what follows is a movement. That's why Southwest employees, at all levels, are politically active. They write letters to Congress or do due diligence on a local municipality before initiating service in a new city. They believe that politics is the business of protecting people's freedom. A piece of legislation that advocates higher landing fees will unleash a ferocious force of resistance. Such a bill is not only detrimental to their bottom line, it's also an affront to their idealism. "If you accept the notion of what Southwest Airlines stands for in terms of this crusade," Ricks said, "then you are going to have a visceral reaction to things that adversely affect your customers."

We recently boarded a Southwest flight from Las Vegas to San Diego. A young woman sat down next to us, pulled out three large law books, and began to study. On the descent into San Diego, we asked, "Are you a law student?"

It is a **heroic** cause that **distinguishes one company** from the next.

"Yes, at the University of San Diego," she answered with a warm, and exhausted, smile. "I live in Las Vegas and perform in the shows at night. I fly to San Diego in the morning for classes, and then fly back in the afternoon. In my first year, I had to do it four times a week; now I'm down to twice. If it wasn't for Southwest's fares and frequency of their flights, I couldn't do it." We were amazed at the young woman's determination. It was also another example of "the business of freedom." Jim Parker, Southwest's vice chairman and CEO, agreed, saying, "This isn't just a business that makes money. What's so exciting about Southwest Airlines is that it is a company that changed the landscape of business in America and continues to change it every time we enter a new market."

The people of Southwest Airlines take "freedom" very seriously. For example, ramp agents know that when they are late by only two minutes to push an aircraft on a morning flight, those two minutes could compound into 90 minutes by the end of the day. They also know that this could mean adding 20 planes to the fleet (at $30 million a piece) to maintain Southwest's schedule. To these "rampers," having to do so is an affront to the business of freedom. But in Southwest's irreverent culture, the concern isn't just criticism from their boss, it's concern for the individual passengers who trust Southwest to get them to their destinations safely and on time.

Sometimes, it is a heroic cause that distinguishes one company from the next. Whereas Kodak and Fuji both manufacture and develop film, Kodak has differentiated itself by turning the customer's need for a solution into the inspiring cause of preserving people's memories. What does MasterCard do that's different from Visa? It enables people to engage in experiences that are priceless. But the difference is more than an advertising spin; it reflects the employees' belief that their work is noble and meaningful. They are helping to create a better world.

A heroic cause is visceral; it comes from the hearts and minds of people who have been moved deeply by the company's purpose. If the image reflected in the cause is instantly apparent, the statement will create an "aha!" moment and you won't have to worry about "buy-in." Here's how some companies have stated their heroic causes:

- *Southwest Airlines:* We are in the freedom business.
- *Apple Computer:* We want to educate the world.
- *Fannie Mae:* We help people achieve the American dream.
- *Medtronic:* We relieve pain, restore health, and give people longer lives.
- *Schwab:* We are the guardians of our customers' financial dreams.
- *SAS:* Giving You the Power to Know.
- *USAA:* Delivering the services and support that makes your life easier and your peace of mind more assured. We're with you.

- *USS* Benfold: We strengthen peace negotiations in the Middle East.
- *Container Store:* We better customers' lives by giving them more time and space.
- *Ernst & Young National Tax Compliance:* Delivering compliance solutions that help our clients succeed by giving them time, freedom, and peace of mind to focus on what's important to them.
- *Monarch High School:* We restore hope and unleash dreams.
- *Freibergs.com:* We tell stories that improve organizations and inspire people to live bigger, better, more fulfilling lives.

By defining your business in heroic terms, you are giving your employees a focus, a beacon, a cause that puts their sometimes humdrum daily work into a larger, ennobling, and engaging perspective.

If ever a heroic cause worked to a business's advantage, it is now. We live in a hyperlinked, 24-hour-a-day world where everyone is swimming, if not drowning, in information and options. Wealth and techno-gadgets have brought us more stress and more discontent, not less. At the same time, business is increasingly managed by women who tend to be more conciliatory, more collaborative, and more compassionate than men. All in all, the typical employee is now likely to welcome and often yearn for more community, meaning, and altruism in the workplace. Give people a crack at something noble and fulfilling, and they will show you a level of dedication and productivity that may well transform your company.

A heroic cause gives you a major competitive advantage. It not only sets your company apart as a unique entity, it also attracts customers who share your cause. In fact, studies have shown that many are willing to pay more for a product if they identify with the company and its cause. That's the kind of loyalty no advertising can buy.

What Makes a Cause Heroic?

What is it about a heroic cause that captivates people's attention, stimulates their interest, and engages them wholeheartedly? What makes it heroic? When we survey companies that are committed to such issues, we find that nearly every cause has certain characteristics:

> Every job productive of any good can be given either a trivial description or a noble description. Ultimate motivation requires that we have in our minds a noble description of what we do!
>
> **—TOM MORRIS**

• **A heroic cause is inspiring.**

Above all else, it's infused with drama, excitement, and emotional appeal. It creates a buzz. It taps into our greatest aspirations, expands our sense of what's possible, and calls us to a more ideal future. It ignites passions, stirs imaginations, raises adrenaline, and unifies people behind a common goal. By giving people something larger than themselves to believe in and strive for, it motivates them to new levels of achievement.

• **A heroic cause connects.**

If the cause is heroic, people will "get it" because they connect with it viscerally. They will be captivated by its inherent goodness. A heroic cause is a tangible expression of one's values, and it speaks to one's vision and hope for a brighter future. People understand it. It

Studies have shown that many are **willing** to **pay more for a product** if they **identify with** the company and **its cause**.

stirs our idealism, which may have been dormant, and anchors it to our daily activities. Many years ago when a member of a tourist group asked Joe Saltzer, a cleaner for the U.S. National Aeronautics and Space Administration, what he did, Joe responded, "I'm helping to put a man on the moon." His view of his heroic cause transforms his ordinary work into a responsibility that awakens the highest levels of passion, enthusiasm, and productivity.

- **Involvement in a heroic cause is rooted in a desire to improve the well-being of others.**

Profitability and the bottom line certainly play a major role, but the ultimate inspiration transcends the numbers. The motivation driving a heroic cause is altruistic. Providing conveniences, eliminating pain and suffering, creating security and peace of mind, transporting goods and materials necessary for society's functioning, and protecting the environment are all about the betterment of the human condition. When we engage in these kinds of activities, we can be assured that our work has meaning and that our lives have not been lived in vain. Our concern for others is an extremely powerful force. It enables us to stay the course when the cause for which we fight gets difficult and burdensome. It intensifies our resolve when others say it can't be done. It can help us overcome our fears when the cause is dangerous.

> The ultimate test of a moral society is the kind of world it leaves to its children.
>
> —**DIETRICH BONHOFFER**

- **A heroic cause is service-oriented.**

What makes a cause heroic is its other orientation. It lifts us out of ourselves and shows us how to put our love for our fellow man into action. It's about what the product, service, or company does to serve others. The Container Store doesn't say it builds the highest-quality shelf units to provide a fair return to its shareholders. It takes something as mundane as plastic containers and closet organizers and makes them exciting. It says, "We better customers' lives by giving them more time and space." In our chaotic, complex world, a company that, say, organizes closets is, in fact, helping people reduce clutter and simplify their lives. Undoubtedly, it provides a service. Within today's intensely competitive marketplace, a business with the goal of solving a problem, instead of gaining market share, will, in the long run, win.

- **A heroic cause is enduring.**

If you work toward a truly heroic goal, your achievements will outlive you. You will be able to look back on your life and know that you made a lasting contribution that, without you, would not exist. Put another way, you're creating your legacy.

- **A heroic cause is authentic.**

Although a heroic cause must be noble and enduring, it must also be an honest statement of what you really do. The cause can't be some slick public-relations or advertising spin. It must have teeth. It must be believable. If it lacks authenticity, employees will write it off as another attempt at manipulation on the part of management. Claiming to care about something you don't care about is pretentious and egotistical. And most often, it is transparent; employees and customers pick up on the hypocrisy right away.

Captain Abrashoff of USS *Benfold* recounted an incident that happened after the first Gulf War when Iraq was unwilling to cooperate with United Nations weapons inspectors. *Benfold* was on very

"Your **combat readiness** and the readiness of *Benfold* has **strengthened peace negotiations** in the Middle East."

high alert in the Persian Gulf and moments away from launching Tomahawk missiles. The tension on the ship was growing as the crew awaited the command to fire. Abrashoff explained that, although

I am certain that after the dust of centuries has passed over our cities, we, too, will be remembered not for our victories or defeats in battle or in politics, but for our contributions to the human spirit.

—JOHN FITZGERALD KENNEDY

launching weapons was something for which the crew had been extensively trained, and though they wanted an opportunity to put their training into practice, everyone also knew that launching these missiles meant killing other human beings. This time, the command never came and the warheads weren't launched. But in his debrief with the crew, Captain Abrashoff said, "Your combat readiness and the readiness of *Benfold* has strengthened peace negotiations in the Middle East." In a moment of nearly unbearable tension, Abrashoff was able to calm the nerves of his crew by repeating his deep-seated belief in the higher cause to which the sailors of *Benfold* were dedicated.

- **A heroic cause is satisfying, and it reveals its presence by the sense of fulfillment people experience when they are engaged with one.**

This doesn't mean it's easy. History shows that people have sacrificed greatly for their causes. Of course, you will feel frustration, anger, disappointment, perhaps even despair when confronting obstacles; still, the satisfaction and pride that comes from pursuing a cause in which you deeply believe will triumph.

Help People Find Themselves in the Cause

A gutsy leader makes an explicit connection between the work people do every day and the larger cause. Dr. Michael DeBakey is one of the foremost heart specialists in the world. He is known not only for his prolific contributions to the medical field, but also as a symbol of hope and encouragement to his colleagues. Many years ago a colleague of ours shadowed Dr. DeBakey for a day at the Methodist Hospital in Houston, Texas. He was struck by DeBakey's capacity to affirm each person he saw in the course of the day. In one particular encounter,

DeBakey began chatting with an elderly janitor who was sweeping the floor. DeBakey asked the man about his wife and children. He told the older man, obviously not for the first time, that the hospital couldn't function without the janitor because germs would spread, increasing the chances of infection in the hospital. Later in the day, our colleague tracked down the janitor and asked him, "What exactly do you do? Tell me about your job." With pride, the janitor replied: "Dr. DeBakey and I? We save lives together." He's right. After all, consider what would happen to our health care systems if the cleaning crews went on strike.

Michael DeBakey understands that the janitor makes a valuable contribution to the hospital's cause. And, even more important, DeBakey understands that showing the janitor exactly how he con-

Gutsy leaders who strive to **motivate others** make time to help people see how **their work** is connected to **something bigger**.

tributes to a larger, more heroic cause is crucial. If this continues, a powerful dynamic can occur. Realizing that he is working toward a worthy goal, the janitor's perceptions about his work change. It has new meaning and his enthusiasm for the job is rejuvenated.

Gutsy leaders who strive to motivate others make time to help people see how their work is connected to something bigger. For a surgeon like DeBakey, those five or ten minutes each day can be costly—unless, of course, you consider the productivity generated by a janitor whose work has been transformed.

Inspired to Greatness

In strong cultures, the heroic cause is part of the daily lives of the people we call heroes. A heroic cause draws its strength from these individuals. They personify its highest ideals and represent its highest values. Heroes are ordinary people who make the routine extraordinary, regardless of their job descriptions or where they sit on the organizational chart. People who bring the best of who they are to work every day inspire others to do the same.

Whether it's making a commitment to a cause like freedom, standing apart from the crowd to embrace a new technology, or the compassion behind astonishing acts of service, heroes put a face on the cause and the qualities we seek in our coworkers. That's why strong cultures are loaded with powerful stories about people who do heroic things. The stories become a kind of self-fulfilling prophecy that draws more people to the cause and inspires more heroic behavior.

What Is the Biggest Payoff?

What happens when an organization's leader gives his or her people a heroic cause—a way to believe that their work contributes to a better world? For one, people may feel more content or relaxed. They become fully engaged mentally, physically, spiritually. And their zeal, of course, translates into financial reward for their companies. Almost by definition, in our experience, a company with a heroic cause attracts purpose driven, heroic people whose dedication translates into impressive profits.

A leader gutsy enough to create a heroic cause surely knows that profit isn't everything, neither for the leader nor for his or her enlightened workers. At the end of the day, helping people become heroes is the essence of gutsy leadership. For leaders, the incomparable payoff is a meaningful life and a chance to leave more than a windblown footprint in the sand.

Jim Goodnight of SAS is such a leader. He and his people really do want to know that at the end of the day what they create actually makes a difference. As an example, he described how SAS aided the U.S. Navy Bureau of Medicine and Surgery, commonly known as BUMED (byew-med).

As the health care provider for the U.S. Navy and Marine Corps, BUMED serves 2.6 million active service members, family members, and retirees through 140 facilities all around the world. It got to a point where there was a huge amount of data from many different types of systems over five levels of geographic hierarchy. Needless to say, BUMED struggled to balance capacity and demand. It needed a software fix that would somehow protect the confidentiality of patient data.

SAS teams worked closely with BUMED to meet those needs, and also to identify places where processes could be optimized. The result? Better use of Navy resources and improved health care for the people who rely on BUMED.

Speaking to a group of senior navy officers, Goodnight described the significance of the project to his workforce: "This means that from our employees' perspective, the software that they write, document, and support is able to make a real difference in people's lives. Fundamentally, people who feel that they can make a difference, will make a difference."

Why Not Try a Collective Response?

Just like an army, a ball club, or any organization, companies need leaders who can define, articulate, and dedicate themselves to a heroic cause. "We've always known that what we stand for, as individuals and as a company, is as important as the ads we create," said GSD&M's Roy Spence. "Do good work and do right by our clients, and we'll do well financially. Do good by our people, they'll do right by us. Do good things for our neighbors, our community, and we'll do well. It never has been a trade-off."

GSD&M's people do a lot of pro bono work, Spence said, because they care about AIDS victims and battered children, about breast cancer, about early-childhood education, about literacy, and about the environment. When skeptics ask, "How do you do all this and still make money?" Spence has a ready answer: "Corporate America doesn't have a choice anymore. People are starting to demand that businesses get involved. Americans are looking beyond the products a company sells to the values that the corporation lives every day." In essence, people are saying, "What you stand for is as important as what you sell," and they're voting at the cash register. Spence went on to say, "The visionary companies—the winners in the marketplace—get involved in the causes that are important to their people and offer their customers the chance to be a part of something bigger, bolder, and more powerful: a collective response."

We believe that there is something inherently noble about what every business does. But let's face it: In some businesses it is more evident than in others. If you're having trouble defining what's heroic about your work, you don't have to deny your people the

Susan Armenta, Executive Director, Monarch High School, working with some students.

opportunity to make a difference. Maybe the place to start is outside your company. Dedicating yourself to a community project and inviting others in your organization to participate can be a huge morale booster.

We, too, believe in making a difference, and we have witnessed the power of what Spence called the collective response. We have been a part of a growing number of San Diego–based entrepreneurs who understand that getting involved in a cause can be a tremendous source of meaning and fulfillment.

Let us introduce you to The Place, which is the result of a collective response in San Diego. It is making a huge difference and has allowed a number of people in a variety of businesses the opportunity to become involved in a heroic cause.

Breaking the Cycle of Poverty at The Place

We know, you think "San Diego" and most people conjure up images of endless sunshine, sandy beaches, a world-famous zoo, and multi-million-dollar houses facing the shimmering Pacific. San Diego bills itself as "America's Finest City," and who's to argue? Well, paradise has an underbelly, a sizable homeless population struggling to survive in the shadow of affluence. Many are victims of alcoholism, drug abuse, and mental illness. Others are casualties of California's severe recession. But saddest of all are the more than 2,500 homeless children who live on the streets of San Diego at any given time.

Without a roof over your head, regular meals, a clean shower, or a place to do homework, going to school becomes futile. When they do show up at school, homeless kids are often ridiculed for wearing the same clothes day after day. Yet education is the only hope most have to break the cycle of poverty. School also provides structure, a hot lunch, friends, and adult role models.

In 1988, a teacher, Sandra McBrayer, set out to make sure these kids weren't forgotten. The first step was renting a small storefront in a dilapidated building in one of downtown San Diego's worst neighborhoods. McBrayer then walked the streets, parks, and shelters, reaching out to homeless children. Out of this came "The Place," an unthreatening school and the first in California for homeless youth. Four years after The Place opened, the U.S. Department of Education named McBrayer America's teacher of the year.

By 1995, The Place was bulging with 70 students crowded into two classrooms. That's when Susan Armenta became principal. From the windows of The Place, she watched the realities of life on the street—students being beaten, stabbed, shot at, even sold—and she came to see her position as much more than a job. She described the experience that changed her life: "I was approaching the school one morning when I noticed a person asleep in our doorway. The figure was curled in on itself for warmth, and I couldn't tell its sex or age. I thought, 'Here we go again, another person I'm going to have to move along so the kids can get into class.' When I reached the doorway, I gently shook the figure's shoulder. The body uncurled, and it was one of my students, a 14-year-old girl who was clutching a textbook in her arms. She sleepily explained that she had a test that morning and was afraid she would miss it. After all, there were no alarm clocks under the freeway, which is where she usually slept. That morning, I swore to myself that I would move mountains to ensure that The Place would be there for her and for all the other kids like her."

Three years later, Armenta's promise was put to the test. The Place lost its lease in a major ballpark redevelopment of the downtown area. Her kids were in jeopardy. Together with several members of San Diego's downtown Rotary, Armenta mobilized members of the business community in what was then a small crusade to save these children's lives and work toward breaking the cycle of poverty.

On the very same day that Armenta learned she lost the lease, Michelle Candland, managing director of CB Richard Ellis, a commercial real-estate firm, walked into The Place. Candland planned to sign on as a mentor, but when Armenta told her that what she really needed was a new school, Candland immediately started looking for a location. The fact that prospective landlords erroneously associated "homeless kids" with drugs and gangs made a hard job nearly impossible. Finally, the group convinced Gordon Menzie, who holds a lot of real estate in San Diego, to visit the school. When he saw the kids at work, Menzie agreed on the spot to sign a long-term lease for an old warehouse that he owned. Located next to a trolley stop in a much better part of downtown San Diego, Menzie's warehouse was in a perfect location. A nonprofit corporation, the Monarch High School Project (www.monarchschools.org) was established, and Armenta was named executive director.

That the group not only triumphed against the odds but achieved remarkable success testifies to the extraordinary results people can attain when they believe they are engaged in work that matters.

"Somebody Else" Won't Solve the Problem

With a location for the new school secured, Bycor General Contractors jumped in and offered to coordinate the construction of the facility pro bono. Bycor's chief executive, Scott Kaats, a volunteer mentor at The Place, was in awe of the fact that these children came to school on their own with no encouragement from parents. With unmistakable admiration, he told us he was "in that school when a 12-year-old girl walked in and did not know her last name. That is almost beyond comprehension for most people. In 12 years, she had never been to school or off her city block, until she came to Monarch. Her job was to pimp for her drug-addicted mother. When you see someone like that reading a month later, using coherent sentence structures a year later, and several years later graduating from high school, it has a very powerful effect on you. To see kids come in bitter and angry and turn that energy into something positive and productive is about as exciting as it gets!"

Kaats observed right away that The Place was surrounded by successful businesses in downtown San Diego, yet lacked the community support it desperately needed. He noted that "as a community we failed that population of kids." Wondering, "Who dropped the ball on this, who let it slide?" Kaats said, "Then it dawned on me, 'There is no "somebody else" . . . to solve this problem.'" Looking down at his feet, Kaats recognized that "the person occupying those shoes must play a role in fixing this problem."

Told We Can't, We Will

In organizations, there are always those who say, "You can't do that." Scott Kaats, and people like him, hear that as a challenge. Gutsy leaders don't easily accept the concept of "no," and they don't do well with bureaucratic red tape. According to Kaats, "Many agencies that could be supporting these kids operate with 'no' too far forward in their modus operandi." When inspired by a heroic cause, "no" becomes just another a bump in the road, not a wall. The Monarch High School Project proved conventional thinkers wrong. Kaats believes that "People want to . . . be involved in something bigger; they just don't know how."

A Cause Draws People Together

Kaats arranged a meeting with another contracting firm so that sub-contractors could learn about the project. At this point, there were no architectural drawings or specific plans; all they had were a vision and a building. Forty contractors showed up, and after hearing the story, every one of them signed on to play a role. As Kaats told us, "Picture a couple of 240-pound, 6-foot-4-inch guys walking up with tears in their eyes, saying, 'We're in; if there is a wire attached to it, consider it taken care of.'" Whether it was for dumpsters, drywall, or civil engineers, the need was addressed. People from all sides of the construction industry, people who usually competed with one another, united to support the cause, which took on a momentum of its own.

Passion for the Cause Creates Acts of Courage

When we asked Kaats about the money, time, and reputation that Bycor was risking with this project, his response was "These kids face the toughest challenges that any . . . on earth face. It's easy to be brave when you've got that in front of you." Shunning accolades for his heroic work at Monarch, he believes that the real heroes are the young people who show up every day when no one's behind them to make them do it. They are heroic because they haven't given up on life. For example, when 14-year-old Charlotte realized she had to get away from her heroin-addicted mother, she took her younger brother and sister with her and got a job. Kaats told us, "She takes care of these kids and puts herself through high school. That takes guts!"

Kaats is convinced that ignoring motivated children is a far greater risk to his business than the time and money he invests in the project. As he told us, "What are we going to lose: a little bit of our time and money—against what? A single life, let alone hundreds of lives." Without help, Kaats explains, "These kids are destined to be unproductive members of society or . . . criminals."

By leveraging Bycor General Contractors' core competence at Monarch, Scott Kaats has given the school the ability to pursue its heroic cause. That this cause, in turn, provides his work with significant meaning is evident when he says, "Every time I walk out of that school, I'm a foot off the ground. This project is like a magnet that draws the best out of people, and the kids are the conduit."

Teach a Person to Fish . . .

Another business leader infected by Armenta's contagious determination to end homelessness is Ralph Rubio, cofounder and chief executive officer of Rubio's Fresh Mexican Grill, a successful restaurant chain famous for its fish tacos. An aficionado of the cuisine of Mexico's Baja peninsula, Rubio convinced his father to finance his first restaurant in 1983. That has grown into a publicly traded company with total revenues of $120 million annually and more than 2,900 employees. The company owns or franchises more than 140 restaurants throughout the western United States.

Susan Armenta wrote to Rubio asking him to cater the school's grand opening. Though he gets many requests for help, Rubio said Armenta's letter "was an awakening moment. . . . A lot of people don't necessarily think of the homeless as children." When he visited The Place, he made a commitment "right there on the spot . . . to help."

Rubio had been thinking of opening a restaurant for a charitable cause for quite some time. After his second visit to The Place, he wondered if the idea of a student-run restaurant in the new location was feasible. From menu design to store layout to marketing, the students would plan everything. The profits would be reinvested in the school to finance college scholarships.

Rubio's idea, enthusiastically endorsed by Susan Armenta, reflected the creativity and guts of a true entrepreneur. Can you imagine making a significant investment in a restaurant that would be owned and run by homeless and at-risk teens? How would you convince the Internal Revenue Service that opening a for-profit business in a nonprofit institution wouldn't cause unfair competition? How do you go about explaining to the board and shareholders of a publicly traded corporation that you are opening a restaurant that will compete with the company's existing units?

Of course, Rubio could have just written a check, but he wanted the students to have "the sense of satisfaction that comes from starting your own business." Susan Armenta, who selected a group of students to work with the team from Rubio's, said, "Ralph immersed himself in the process. He was genuinely interested in what the kids had to say."

After the students helped name the restaurant Cabo Café, Armenta helped them establish its decor. They cut out pictures from magazines that they thought aesthetically represented the restaurant. The pictures were turned into a collage that served as the basis for working with Rubio's in-house designer, Ann Casadont. Rubio explained, "There were times when I had to pull our people back. They certainly had the expertise to come up with the name, menu, and design for the restaurant. I said, 'Wait, let the students come back to us with their recommendations.' I wanted the students to drive the process, and I wanted it to be a very interactive learning experience."

The Compounded Effect of a Cause

The spirit of working on a heroic cause has a compounding effect on individuals, drawing like-minded people with different competencies into a team. Just as Scott Kaats was able to mobilize contractors, Ralph Rubio attracted many of his vendors to the project. Coca-Cola and Starbucks provided beverages and equipment; Jack-in-the-Box built the school's kitchen; and Rubio's financial advisers, Creative Capital Management, Inc., handled the complicated tax issues, aided by the law firm of Brobeck, Phleger & Harrison.

In his passion to save these kids, Rubio followed the saying "If you give a person a fish, you feed them for a day. If you teach a person to fish, you feed them for a lifetime." The money they earn working in the restaurant is what enables many of the students to come to Monarch. As Susan Armenta pointed out, "When they first arrive, [they are dealing with] survival; many . . . are forced to choose between having a job, possibly supporting younger brothers or sisters, and going to school. Having a restaurant on-site enables them to do both."

Over half of the restaurant's 18 employees are Monarch students who work hand-in-hand with Rubio's managers. At Cabo Café, they develop a sense of responsibility, establish a résumé, gain work experience, and learn about running a business firsthand. Most important of all, according to Rubio, they gain pride and self-confidence. "Many of these kids don't own all that much," Rubio said, "and I made it very clear to them that they own this restaurant. Nobody else does. When they see the sales grow and the business becomes more successful year after year, there's a lot of pride in that."

Inspired by Susan Armenta, other San Diego businesspeople, such as Peter Van Horne, have rolled up their sleeves. Van Horne, one of the first developers of high-speed Internet access, sold his company to Cisco Systems, then went to work there. At a planning meeting for Monarch, he asked Armenta, "What needs has nobody stepped up for yet?" When she shared her vision of a state-of-the-art computer lab, Van Horne pulled out a small pad of paper, made some notes, and said, "I'll take care of that." Silence fell over the room. Concerned that he didn't understand the magnitude of the project, Armenta came up with a long list of the equipment that would be needed. Van Horne didn't blink. On move-in day, he and 20 colleagues showed up and equipped a 20-station computer lab, including furniture and a big-screen projector. As Van Horne assembled computer furniture,

Armenta asked him about his dream job. Van Horne responded, "I'm doing it now."

The Monarch High School Project is a powerful example of what can happen when a gutsy leader captures people's attention, ignites imaginations, and stirs hearts. Over and over in our research, we have seen people eager to connect with something greater than themselves, something to which they can devote their time, talents, and energy—in short, a heroic cause.

Building a world-class organization—a school for homeless children or a multinational corporation—requires a wellspring of passion and conviction that lies dormant in many people. Gutsy leaders know that a heroic cause unleashes this hidden power. It ignites devotion that enables people to overcome obstacles and accomplish extraordinary things. In this case, a worthy cause connected a number of gutsy leaders from all corners of the community together. Everyone involved senses that something miraculous is under way, and it continues to attract unprecedented and much-needed attention and involvement.

The poet Robert Frost once said, "Isn't it a shame that when we get up in the morning our minds work furiously—until we come to work." Sadly, many employees are bored, alienated, or stressed and simply go through the motions of their jobs. Their work lives lack spirit, joy, and significance because they feel no connection with a larger and heroic cause. If you can define what you do as a force for good in the world, and if you can communicate that cause, your organization can develop an unstoppable esprit de corps. Your people will view their work as a crusade that contributes to a better world. They will bring more than their bodies to work; they will readily engage with their minds, their hearts, and their spirits.

Out of the Cocoon

After an initial contribution of $50,000 from the San Diego Padres Wives Foundation, more than $1 million was raised and work started on a new building. It opened in the spring of 2001, renamed Monarch High School by its students, in honor of the butterfly's journey from its dark, restricting cocoon to the sunlight where it spreads its wings and flies.

When children first come to Monarch, some are given medical checkups (which may be their first doctor visits), as well as shoes, clothing, and baby formula and diapers if necessary. Then their literacy levels are assessed and a baseline for their educational needs is established. In just the few days it takes to perform these basic measures, Armenta explained, you can see the children's self-esteem increase. After all, they are getting a small dose of the care, attention, and love that every child needs to grow and blossom.

Today, Monarch High School is a collective response. The children are taught and mentored by people from nearly every segment of San Diego's diverse population, including business leaders, professional athletes, professors and teachers, and students from other schools. Musicians and artists share their gifts and help the students discover and express their creativity. In addition, volunteer psychologists and physicians are always available. The building buzzes with energy, purpose, compassion, love, and hope.

One reason it all works so well is the school's tough-love philosophy. In Armenta's words, "We offer hope in the form of an education, a safe place within which to learn, grow, and heal, but with that comes responsibility; the kids have to meet us halfway, they have to want to make better lives for themselves, and they have to work for it. That means staying clean, showing up with a good attitude, doing their homework, and participating in at least one extracurricular activity."

Graduation ceremonies at Monarch are often deeply moving. One young, frightened boy, who has grown up on the streets, graduates after five months at Monarch High School. He has worked hard to learn, build an identity, and begin to find a place for himself in the world. Now a young man, he stands in front of a hushed auditorium and delivers a stirring valedictorian address that earns him cheers and tears. Armenta pointed out, "We've broken the cycle of poverty in [many] . . . families." Last year, Monarch graduated twelve students. One has been accepted at the University of California at Berkeley; ten others are working and attending community college. Eleven are no longer homeless; Armenta has lost contact with one. Eleven more students graduated in 2003 with hopes and dreams of creating a better life.

Monarch High School has become a catalyst and a beacon for the entire city. It is a tribute to the diversity and gifts of its student body, to the generosity and caring of San Diego's citizenry, and to the grit and guts of Susan Armenta. Today, because Monarch's population continues to grow, those involved with the high school are trying to raise money to renovate two additional buildings across the street from the school. If the school is successful, these buildings will house a new high school, leaving the current facility open for a new elementary school. New volunteers continually come forward and are always welcome. Everyone is drawn toward work that matters. As David S. Pottruck, co–chief executive officer of Charles Schwab, once noted, "People will work hard for money, but they will devote their lives to meaning."

✓ **Is it a job or a life's work?** A job is where we temporarily put in time in order to be paid. A life's work usually transcends the temporal and is what some people refer to as a "calling." Challenge yourself and others by asking: Am I just working at a job or am I engaged in my life's work?

✓ **Find your heroic cause:** Consider the value your products and services bring to the world. What is heroic about what your organization does, even if it appears to be mundane—say, making nails, delivering food, or cleaning bathrooms? Perhaps those nails hold together houses within which live people's dreams; that food you deliver provides sustenance and pleasure; and cleaning bathrooms improves public health.

In 1991, Fannie Mae, the country's largest source of mortgage funds, came to GSD&M for advice on how to reach low- to moderate-income families.

GSD&M developed a campaign called "Opening Doors," with the goal of presenting Fannie Mae as a partner that is ready to guide people through the complexities of finding and financing a house. Opening Doors included multilingual advertising, seminars, booklets, and one-on-one counseling designed to demystify the daunting and, for many, intimidating process.

GSD&M helped Fannie Mae redefine itself. Until then, Fannie Mae viewed itself as part of the secondary mortgage market. Now, it wasn't "just lending money anymore," it was in the business of helping people achieve the American Dream. It was "making a real difference in the lives of hard-working people," as one GSD&M executive told us. In just five years, Opening Doors generated more than 10 million inquiries.

✓ **Deepen your ideas:** If you need help identifying your heroic cause, ask employees how they explain their work to their children. You might be surprised by the depth and sincerity of their answers. Deepen the dialogue by repeatedly asking "why" after each response. For example, if you were Southwest Airlines, you might have the following exchange:

Question: Why do we exist?

Answer: To provide safe, efficient air travel to the short-haul, high-frequency, point-to-point market with incredible service.

Question: Why is that important?

Answer: People rely on us to get them where they are going.

Question: Why is that important?

Answer: People who couldn't afford to fly before are now able to go, and, as a result, have extraordinary experiences.

Question: For example?

Answer: A grandparent on a limited income can visit his family more often. The child of divorced parents can see each more often. The entrepreneur expanding her business from one city to another can now afford to visit more customers.

Question: What do you conclude?

Answer: Our goal is not only to move people from point A to point B; we are in the business of freedom.

✓ **Express your cause in words:** Gutsy leaders know that words can stir the heart and ignite the spirit. When Winston Churchill said, "We shall fight on the beaches, we shall fight on the landing grounds, we shall fight in the fields and in the streets, we shall fight in the hills; we shall never surrender," people felt inspired to fight for freedom. As you craft how you will phrase your cause, keep these ideas in mind:

• Be audacious. The power of a heroic cause lies in its audacity. Saying that you are going to do what you can to change the world is gutsy enough to draw criticism or ridicule. Yet, gutsy leaders don't dilute their language for any reason.

• Be authentic. Today more than ever, people are offended by slick talk. Make sure that what you do does indeed define the cause, and that the cause reflects what you actually do. You must represent it, not just mouth it.

• Don't assign a committee the job of drafting the words of your heroic cause unless you want to weaken its authority and diminish its provocative power. In other circumstances, people may be more likely to assume responsibility for the cause if they contributed to shaping its verbal expression, but that will be negated in this case. By trying to please everyone and offend no one, committee members are likely to produce a statement so lacking in passion that they will be the only ones wishing to pursue it.

• Remember, a heroic cause does not emerge from the intellect. It comes from the heart of someone who has been deeply moved. If possible, offer him or her the opportunity to verbally communicate its meaning. His or her words will be those most likely to evoke an "aha!" moment in others.

✓ Help people find their place in the cause:

Allocate a few days to visit your employees, especially those engaged in routine, repetitive work. Ask yourself if they seem engaged in their jobs or appear drugged by the monotony of the mundane. Then make an explicit connection between the work they do every day and the crusade for which your company fights. The fellow running the forklift at a Kodak warehouse needs to be reminded that he is helping people preserve the most important moments of their lives.

Keep the cause front and center at all times. It is one thing to deliver a speech, outlining your heroic cause, that leaves people excited and motivated. And it is quite another to keep them committed once the initial enthusiasm fades. Of course, there will be times when the daily issues of running a company supersede all else and both you and your people lose sight of the cause. Gutsy leaders never let this go on for long. If you want people to feel like heroes, periodically remind them how their individual contributions are supporting a cause, the meaning of which extends beyond themselves.

✓ Establish a direct line of sight between your employees and your customers: Imagine a plant
that builds a Doppler system that enables the Apache helicopter to navigate in pitch darkness. What if a person on the assembly line had an opportunity to hear an Apache pilot describe what goes through his or her mind when that system fails in the heat of combat? Odds are good that the factory worker would develop a new, more heroic perspective about his or her job. Employees whose direct line of sight is the customer will feel more committed to, passionate about, and creative in their work.

CHAPTER 7

Gutsy Leaders
Inspire Fun

Let's face it: Life just isn't always fun. It's gotten so fast, so complex, and so busy that doing anything out of the ordinary, like switching a bank account or shopping for a car, can ratchet up the stress level.

But wait—hold on a minute. Buying a car can actually be fun—if you're buying it from Planet Honda, a car dealership in Union, New Jersey. Planet Honda is transforming the customer's purchasing experience, turning it from taxing to terrific, from woeful to wonderful, from excruciating to exciting, from . . . well, you get the idea.

Fun Pays!

Take everything you like seriously, except yourselves.

—RUDYARD KIPLING

Planet Honda's chief executive officer and driving spirit, Tim Ciasulli, is a man who understands that making work fun isn't limited to pranks, jokes, and outrageous parties. Work is fun when people are living their dreams, training to become competent in their field, and developing an important relationship with an employer who shows a genuine interest in their development. Planet Honda employees have plenty of wild and crazy fun, but at the heart of Ciasulli's mission is his deep belief that personal fulfillment is also fun.

For the customers, the fun starts in the parking lot, where a walking, talking lemon with the international "no" sign—Planet Honda's mascot—greets people with a message that's anything but sour: "No lemon on the lot! If for any reason you feel that you bought a lemon at Planet Honda, we'll completely refund your money or give you a new car." In his 30 years of selling cars, Ciasulli has been asked only once to make good on the offer.

We spent one intriguing afternoon watching people experience this atypical showroom. Here are a few ways in which it declares its uniqueness. First, the air is treated with aromatherapy to oxygenate the blood, stimulate the senses, and create a relaxing atmosphere. The entire showroom, including the palm trees, is designed to help people forget their woes, escape their ordinary routines, and enjoy the ambience that quietly announces that buying a car at Planet Honda can be an exhilarating experience.

Ciasulli believes in empowering the customer. That means no aggressive salespeople descend upon you the moment you drive into the lot. Instead, people are welcomed by a receptionist, who asks, "Welcome, how can we help you?" When the answer is "We're just looking," as it generally is, the receptionist hands customers a map and encourages them to explore any and every part of the dealership that interests them. Then comes a touch that we consider genius: All "just-looking" customers are given small yellow badges (a "happy face") that read "J.L."—for "just looking." As long as they are wearing that badge, no salesperson will approach them.

Ciasulli told us, "People are very defensive when they walk into a car dealership. Many have had awful experiences in the past. And remember, outside of a house, a car is the most expensive item most people ever buy. My customers work hard for their money—I have a deep respect for that.

"What's really amazing," he continued, "is that after about 15 or 20 minutes . . . most people will go up to a salesperson and ask, 'Geez, what's the coefficient of drag on this new Accord?' Of course, they [customers] know the answer because they've done their homework. Honda customers are pretty bright." The salespeople, however, completely respectful of the "just-looking" policy, politely ask the customers to remove their "J.L." badges before further discussing the merchandise. According to Ciasulli, "The moment they peel off that sticker, they're ready to get serious about buying a car from us. They've been empowered."

Planet Honda's "Just Looking" Badge.

That is why we call it genius. Who's in charge? The customer. Who sets the agenda? The customer. Who's given the respect? The customer.

Those customers who are not yet ready to take off the sticker can research the cars on the Internet while sipping a free cappuccino at the Tech Café. In his attempt to make a visit to Planet Honda as agreeable as possible, Ciasulli built Kid's Corner, which is stocked with video games, Legos, books, and new friends. With the kids

A glimpse of Planet Honda's Tech Café.

entertained, buying a car becomes a relaxed and, for most people, a brand-new experience.

If you're not shopping, but waiting for your car, your experience at Planet Honda will still be different. You can head for the quiet room, where you can plug in your laptop and work. Or, if you're a woman interested in learning how to change a flat tire, check your tire pressure, or check your oil, you can view a session of WOW—Women on Wheels. If you head to the women's room, you find fresh-cut flowers. What's the magic of the Ciasulli show? To surprise, delight, and empower even the most jaded and demanding customers.

Ciasulli instinctively understands something that too many of us forget: Fun is a brilliant business tool. He explained to us: "There's nothing unique about our product. Our distinction is the customer experience. Simply stated, we believe in fun. That's why we use aromatherapy. We developed a proprietary blend that produces a feeling of abundance and joy while stimulating the immune system. Fredric's Corporation has been using aromatherapy in its facility for years. Holzberger uses energizing aromas in the child development center during play time and relaxing aromas during nap time. Casinos pump in a ton of oxygen after midnight so that people will stay up and gamble. I've heard that Nordstrom does the same thing in some of its high-end boutiques."

> If I were given an opportunity to present a gift to the next generation, it would be the ability for each individual to learn to laugh at himself.
> —CHARLES SHULTZ

Ciasulli is always on the lookout for new ways to make the customer's experience fun. On a trip to Palo Alto, California, Ciasulli and his wife stopped in a teahouse. He was amazed to discover that it offered 300 varieties of tea. Knowing how aromatherapy produces a feeling of abundance and joy while stimulating the immune system, Ciasulli asked the owner if he had a tea that would put someone in the proper state of mind for buying a car. The owner asked, "What state are you trying to induce?" And Ciasulli replied, "Desire." The owner said he had just the thing, oolong tea, brewed from leaves handpicked by monkeys along the cliffs of Chinese rivers. It also happened to be the most expensive tea in the store.

Now, when a salesperson can't close a deal at Planet Honda, he or she will say to the manager, "Mr. Jones wants to go home and talk to his wife." The manager will say, "Well, what time is it?" The well-coached salesperson will respond: "It's tea time!" Then they will have a good laugh with Mr. Jones over a cup of oolong tea, regaling him with the story of the tea picked by monkeys that ignites desire. "People love it," Ciasulli said. "The women want the tea for their husbands, the husbands want the tea for their wives, and it's very, very funny. It's like a 100-percent closing ratio with the tea."

Located in Planet Honda's showroom is an 18-foot spaceship simulator that seats four people and creates a half G-force.

Planet Honda is so much fun that many customers like to hang out while their cars are being serviced. So Ciasulli has built a theater in the basement where customers can relax in plush leather chairs and watch movies on their own personal screens while munching on free popcorn.

An inspired and inspiring gutsy businessman, Ciasulli understands that buying a new car is a major event for most people, and Planet Honda treats it that way. Once they've signed the papers, customers enjoy a celebration that culminates with a trip aboard a $150,000 simulator, an 18-foot spaceship located right in the showroom. Like a ride airlifted from Disney World, it thrills, excites, educates, and unites. Mom, Dad, and the kids, strapped into their seats, blast off for a virtual, wild trip to Planet Honda, nearly colliding with an asteroid on the way. When they land at Planet Honda, a welcoming person dressed in a spacesuit appears and explains their owner's manual, maintenance schedule, and warranty. Then Ciasulli comes on the screen, thanks them for their purchase, and reinforces the dealership's commitment to its customers, the community, and the environment. If Ciasulli wants buyers to leave Planet Honda feeling completely enamored of it, this eight-minute ride is the perfect parting adventure.

Ciasulli's use of fun as a key competitive weapon has differentiated his company from all others. Not just customers, but employees and managers, have a better time, and the company achieves spectacular results.

- The average amount of time between the decision to buy a car, completion of all the necessary paperwork, and the actual delivery of the vehicle to the customer has been slashed from an average of 3 hours to 40 minutes.
- Planet Honda used to spend $450 per car in advertising. It now spends one-third of that, because much of its business comes from word of mouth.

"It's like a 100-percent closing ratio with the tea."

- In an industry notorious for a high turnover rate among salespeople, Planet Honda's annual turnover is less than 1 percent.
- The company sold more than 4,000 new Hondas and 2,000 previously owned vehicles in 2002—400 percent more than did the average Honda dealer. And almost 50 percent of those sales came from repeat customers or word-of-mouth referrals from happy buyers.
- Planet Honda has opened a dealership in Passaic Park, New Jersey, and has plans to expand further into Florida, Pennsylvania, and South Carolina.
- Amazingly, customers can get all of this fun, superior service, and an experience that blows the doors off car-buying-as-usual for the same price they would pay elsewhere . . . bottom line, it costs Ciasulli no more to deliver greatness.

Fun Pays

Far too many managers believe that fun and business aren't compatible. And they pay a price both professionally and personally. When we visit somber, uptight organizations that discourage fun, we consistently find low morale and productivity. More important, once customers experience the stifling environment, they tend to take their business elsewhere. Many people are trapped by what our friend and colleague, Moose Millard, calls "the tyranny of the 'or.'" Within this "either/or" logic, we can be either professional or lighthearted; be profitable or love people; be productive or have fun. Yet evidence suggests otherwise. Companies run by the gutsy leaders we have studied embrace "the genius of 'and.'" These organizations have stronger morale, higher recruitment and retention rates, superior levels of productivity and customer satisfaction, and greater profitability—and feature fun on the job.

You can sense the difference the minute you walk in the door.

Whereas each of these companies has its own culture, they all share a spirit of hospitality and aliveness; you know immediately that people are genuinely glad to see you; their smiles aren't forced, and they feel free to express their unique personalities.

Needless to say, organizations such as Quad/Graphics, which must meet critical deadlines, and Southwest Airlines, which is responsible for safely transporting more than 500,000 customers a day, or a leader like the Navy's Captain Mike Abrashoff, who guided USS *Benfold* through the Persian Gulf, know how to take their businesses seriously.

He who does not get fun and enjoyment out of every day . . . needs to reorganize his life.

—GEORGE MATTHEW ADAMS

But for these leaders and their successful enterprises, fun is a core business strategy that doesn't interfere with seriousness. In fact, it complements it, which gives these organizations and their leaders a distinct advantage over competitors who see fun as peripheral or even counterproductive.

Roy Spence, GSD&M's president, takes his sense of fun, and his refusal to take himself too seriously, wherever he goes—even to a shareholders' meeting of its client Wal-Mart. "It was a dark and stormy night in Bentonville," began Troy Walker, an account supervisor at GSD&M. The "meeting was scheduled for 6:30 the next morning. All of us except Roy showed up in the lobby bright and early the next day, along with representatives from Procter & Gamble, Coca-Cola, Lever Brothers, Pennzoil, and quite a few other *Fortune* 500 companies. At 5:30 A.M., in front of a lobby filled with corporate executives, Roy strolled in wearing a dress shirt, tie, shiny black cowboy boots, and his boxer shorts. 'Has anybody seen my pants?'

"For a minute no one said a word. Then the laughter broke out. 'Could these be your pants?' asked the slightly embarrassed desk clerk. 'They were out in the parking lot.' They had apparently fallen off a hanger the night before and were dripping wet.

"Completely undaunted, Roy held up the wet pants. 'Got a blow dryer?' Much to the delight of the growing crowd in the lobby, Roy plugged the dryer in and went to work on those pants. In a few minutes he had britches dry enough to wear. We went on to have a great meeting that day. More important, I learned that Roy Spence truly has no fear, and that a willingness to laugh at yourself can get you through just about any situation."

There are a number of hardheaded business benefits to be gained from having fun in your work life. Let's take them each in turn.

Fun Differentiates Your Company

Fun sets you apart from the crowd and gives you an identity that makes your competition seem boring. Because people pay attention to humor, your message is more likely to be remembered.

Don't forget the improvements in Planet Honda's numbers once fun became part of its standard operating procedure. Its advertising costs decreased by two-thirds. That means that the company no longer has to spend money in the media to make its quality known, and that it's benefiting from the very best kind of advertising: word of mouth.

Fun Attracts Customers

Offering fun gives your people and your customers a gift. When the challenges of life threaten to overwhelm us, we look for, and are grateful to find, comic relief. It's clear at Planet Honda—everyone loves to do business with people who are fun.

Southwest is another business that creates a fun environment. Gate agents play games with customers. So do flight attendants. Among the favorites: the Biggest Hole in Your Sock Award. Also, the next time you're on one of Southwest's flights, pay attention to the quality of the sounds around you; you'll hear chatter and animated, lighthearted conversation, reflecting people's engagements with one another. Then notice the absence of that noise on other commercial flights, where people are working, sleeping, or simply keeping to themselves, not socializing with each other.

Fun Fosters Trust and Levels Hierarchy

Leaders who laugh at themselves are able to disarm others, creating an immediate rapport with them. Suddenly, such leaders are seen as human, with their foibles on display. Fun frees people to be authentic, and instantly diminishes the usual anxieties of dealing with higher-ups. It's hard to feel fearful, rigid, hostile, or inflexible when you laugh. Humor, in other words, opens the channels of communication and increases trust.

One leader we interviewed who understood the uses of fun was the recently departed and sorely missed Harry Quadracci. Another is Southwest's Herb Kelleher. Quadracci always discouraged his managers from taking themselves too seriously. In fact, he actually imposed a program of "forced fun." Once a year, he threw dignity to the wind and produced the "Management Revue," an irreverent musical for the entertainment of Quad's thousands of employees. Quadracci told us the show was "a way of glueing the company together. Once you get up and make an ass of yourself in front of [thousands of] people, what else is left?" The event breaks down barriers and frees managers to experiment with new ideas without fearing ridicule or failure.

I want flying to be a helluva lot of fun! Life is too short and too hard and too serious not to be humorous about it.

—HERB KELLEHER

An annual Quad ritual since 1981, the revue is perhaps the most anticipated event of the year. To compare the scale of the revue to a

Harry Quadracci had no problem performing for his people at Quad's annual management revues, including riding his Harley through the plant with his wife, Betty.

Vegas event is hardly an exaggeration. The cast rehearses for eight weeks, and the production requires four semitrailer trucks to haul in the sets and lighting. Harry Quadracci captured the spirit of the event when he told his employees, "You perform for us throughout the year. This is our opportunity to perform for you."

Herb Kelleher, who is famous for his lack of pretentiousness, has an enviable ability to laugh at himself. Once, when Colleen Barrett, Kelleher's successor as president of Southwest, walked into a packed meeting and brusquely told him, "Herbie, get your coat," Kelleher turned to the group and said, "That either means I'm cold or I'm going somewhere."

> "You **perform for us** throughout the year. This is **our opportunity** to **perform for you.**"

Another leader who likes to keep things light is the loved, respected, and self-effacing Ray Marcy, the former chief executive of Spherion. A brilliant businessman, Ray appreciates a good joke and is always willing to poke fun at himself. As a result, he has been the target of numerous pranks at work. The day after he arrived home from a long European trip, Marcy was scheduled to attend an important board meeting. His executive team decided to lighten it up. Since he is a necktie connoisseur, members of the team arranged with his wife to come over, raid his closet, and confiscate 25 ties as soon as he left the house that morning. At the meeting, each male executive gave his presentation sporting a tie from the "Ray Marcy Collection." Every member of the executive team bet on how long it would take him to notice. It took the jet-lagged Marcy almost two hours. At last, he stood up, took a long hard look around, burst into laughter, and said, "Hey, you're all wearing my damn ties."

Another time, Marcy heard some commotion in the parking lot outside his office. When he looked out the window, he quickly realized that the excitement had something to do with his brand-new Jaguar. It turned out that his employees had acquired the keys and were auctioning off the car for the weekend to the highest bidder.

Stories like this are legion among Spherion employees. Roy Marcy knows that you can't legislate fun, you have to live it.

Fun Stimulates Creativity

Fun enhances creativity, curiosity, imagination, initiative, and mental agility in the marketplace. Humor can relieve tension and turn a frustrating meeting into a productive one. Fun has a way of helping us loosen up and ignore the self-doubt that can stifle spontaneity.

When Synovus undertook a massive information-technology system conversion at more than 40 affiliated banks, it used humor to lighten up the daunting undertaking. The new system was called TIPS—Technology Improving Personal Service—and a TIPS troupe traveled to every bank to host a crazy casting call. The TIPS team recruited employees at each bank to play roles in a skit designed to teach everyone about the conversion, its timeline, and the reasons for doing it. There were executives in miniskirts, grandmas with pom-poms, and employees dancing in the aisles. TIPS chips were given out for attending these parties and could be cashed in for various prizes. At the conclusion of each bank's successful conversion, every employee received a $100 tip.

> Sustained laughter stimulates an increased release of endorphins—the body's own natural morphine. We feel better when we laugh because endorphins actually diminish physical and psychological pain. Endorphins also stimulate the body's immune system to increase its disease-fighting ability.
>
> **—NORMAN COUSINS**

Elizabeth James, Synovus's vice chairman and chief information officer, said, "We really wanted to look these folks in the eye at the end of this deal and say, 'Look, even $100 is not enough, but it's a token of our appreciation for everything you did.'" TIPS team members reported that the goodwill and shared laughs made the hard

◄ THE TIPSTER
Our mascot for the conversion to the new bank. This lovable character will travel to every affiliate, helping team members make the change to our new system. Humor always helps!

work that followed a lot easier for them and the employees learning the new system. By making a challenging assignment fun, they gave people the freedom to laugh, and "ha-ha"s often lead to insightful new "ah-ha"s. Fun and laughter will almost always provide a new lens through which to consider and approach a difficult situation.

Here's a surprising example from Alan Kline and Eric Wolf, two senior partners of Ernst & Young's National Tax Compliance Group, who rolled out a new connectivity program with flair rarely exhibited by tax accountants. They produced a videotape of themselves sitting at a desk in a hotel room reviewing facts and figures on a computer screen. This was the dialogue:

Eric: "I really thought that was a great meeting today."

Alan: "Me too, Eric. In fact, I'm really excited about all that we've accomplished in Tax Compliance."

Eric: "Alan, it's been a long day. I'm ready to hit the hay."

The two men stand up and remove their blazers, revealing that they're in their pajamas and ready for bed. They walk over to the bed.

Eric: "Boy, I know the firm is trying to cut down on costs, but I never thought it would come to this."

Alan: "But hey, at least they let us get a king bed this time!"

Together the two get into bed and pull the covers up.

The video was so surprising and hilarious that it was shown to 700 uproariously laughing partners at a firm-wide meeting.

Fun Reduces Conflict

People who play and laugh together are more likely to resolve conflicts more quickly and painlessly, because laughter releases tension.

Harry Quadracci told us a story that perfectly illustrates this point—that laughter can defuse a tense situation to such a degree that, for Quadracci, it salvaged an important deal. A meeting between Quadracci and *Newsweek* magazine's Angelo Rivello, the magazine's senior vice president of manufacturing, had gotten very heated over a relatively minor issue. The session ran late and ended with the men cursing each other. A follow-up meeting was scheduled for the next morning. While Rivello was shaving, he found a box of Band-Aids in the medicine cabinet and had an inspiration. Before he could talk himself out of it, he shared his idea with his team, all of whom covered their faces with bandages and walked into the meeting, wearing mementos of the "fight" the night before. As soon as he looked at them, Quadracci burst into uncontrollable laughter. The two teams embraced, exchanged apologies for their mutually immature behavior the night before, and began a friendship that now spans more than a quarter of a century.

Fun Acts as a Retention Magnet

Everyone loves to laugh and have fun. So, if it is known that good times are part of the cultural fabric of your company, job seekers are more likely to sign up—and then hold on to a good thing.

Ray Marcy seems to have time for fun no matter what else is going on. When Marcy was at the helm of Spherion, some sort of prank to entertain new hires during their culture training was a company tradition. Gary Peck, former president of worldwide staffing, remembers being interrupted in the middle of a meeting by someone who announced: "You're coming with us!" Escorted to a room where he found Marcy and two inflatable sumo wrestling suits, he and Marcy were instructed to suit up. "We're going to blow you up and take you down to the lobby for the wrestling match of your lives," they were told. As soon as the two were fully inflated and feeling like full-blown idiots, they were taken down in separate glass elevators. By the time they reached the third floor, the two sumo "wrestlers" were visible to the crowd below, who let out a cheer. When the doors opened in the lobby, the crowd of hundreds of employees and lots of kids—it happened to be bring-your-child-to-work day—went wild.

With the *Rocky* theme song blaring, Marcy and Peck became the afternoon's entertainment. They were cheered, laughed at, knocked down, picked up, dusted off, and laughed at some more through four rounds of hysteria. The spoof made the local newspaper and, more important, raised money for a local charity; for $1, you could have your picture taken with one of the wrestlers and bring home a sumo souvenir. It was interesting, too, for the kids to see the lighter side of Spherion and of serious business in general. And, as Marcy intended, another group of new hires learned that Spherion takes play seriously.

Youth is not a period of time. It is a state of mind, a result of the will, a quality of the imagination, a victory of courage over timidity, of the taste of adventure over the love of comfort. A man doesn't grow old because he has lived a certain number of years; he grows old when he deserts his ideal. The years may wrinkle his skin, but deserting his ideal wrinkles his soul.

—GENERAL DOUGLAS MACARTHUR

Phil Dean, who runs one of the most successful Stanley Steemer franchises in the nation, has a more straightforward approach to

And in the end, it's not the years in your life that count. It's the life in your years.

—ABRAHAM LINCOLN

fun. "We gear our celebrations toward concrete symbols of recognition. We have a big dinner, and we give out about 25 awards, for everything from highest sales to safety to efficiency to scheduling. Most of them have never won anything before in their lives. The pride in their faces is something to behold. Everyone else is on their feet clapping and cheering. After the awards we have dancing—just a big fat party [that] works for our company."

Fun Circumvents Boredom and Burnout

Boredom, anxiety, and stress are estimated to cost U.S. business billions of dollars a year. But clever and committed leaders can break this deadly cycle. For example, Mike Abrashoff told us that, in order to test USS *Benfold*'s fire safety, obviously a critical task, a series of routine drills had to be repeated month after month.

In an attempt to make them fun and keep people alert and on their toes, Abrashoff instituted the "Fire Drill Olympics." Teams were pitted against one another in exciting events, such as "Roll Out and Position Hoses" and "Lower the Lifeboats." As a result, mundane tasks were transformed into games that were fun and had variety. Not incidentally, the crew's skills were honed, so they got the job done more quickly.

Garth Brooks, one of the best-selling recording artists of all time, told Kevin that performing 160 concerts a year becomes tedious. When the band grows stale, Garth assigns a band member a new job—the drummer will play keyboards or nonsingers will sing, for example. Garth said, "Now they're embarrassed, and they sound horrid. I mean horrid! But three or four bars into it, they're laughing and having a good time. It creates . . . a healthy fear, and they start to find their game." It takes courage and confidence to deliberately jeopardize the quality of a performance, but that is precisely why leaders have to be gutsy and innovative. When people go on automatic pilot, which in Abrashoff's case can be life-threatening, you can jolt them out of it by doing something outrageously different and fun.

Fun Is Just Plain Healthy

Laughter stimulates the immune system, increases the secretion of beta endorphins (the body's natural painkillers), and exercises the cardiovascular and respiratory systems. As our heart rate increases, oxygenated blood feeds the entire body, including the brain. We think more clearly, feel less distracted, and learn more readily. In addition, laughter relaxes the muscles and relieves stress and anxiety. According to Dr. William J. Fry of the Stanford University Medical School, "Humor is contagious. Laughter is infectious. Both are good for your health."

Recently, Jackie had a poignant experience that shows us how relevant and important Dr. Fry's advice about humor really is. She gave a presentation to an insurance group in Nebraska, which was warmed up by a comedian, David Naster, who shared an experience with the insurance group. He had been invited to perform for a group of midwestern farmers, yet he had no idea what farmers considered funny. To his credit, he spent two days with a few real farmers, getting to know them and the challenges and satisfactions of their work. His effort paid off. Those farmers laughed long and hard just when he hoped they would, and even when he didn't expect it. After the event, Naster was thrilled, having reaffirmed that making people laugh was his calling. As he was leaving, one farmer took him aside and confided, "Nine months ago, we lost our baby girl. . . . I didn't think I would ever be okay, and I didn't know if I would ever laugh again. But tonight . . . you made me laugh, and now I know I'm going to be okay." On that night in Nebraska, Jackie learned that you don't have to be happy to laugh; laughing makes you happy.

Now, if you buy into the idea that having fun is good business, the question becomes: How do you integrate it into your organization's culture? If play comes naturally for some, for others it causes discomfort. And for many of us who have grown older and taken on more responsibilities, fun seems to have faded from our day. But that doesn't mean that even the most serious of us can't lighten up and look for the lighter side of life.

Find Your Recipe for Fun

Do you have the guts to set fun free within your company? It's a given—you need your people to perform; but to do that well, they need a lot more than earnest exhortations. "That's it—we're going to have more fun around here!" generally doesn't work. People need to be given the freedom to have fun and the freedom to express their individual gifts of humor on the job. What we've learned is you can't legislate people to have fun, but your own willingness to participate in it demonstrates the importance you place on fun. Why not try it—don't just commit to fun, get involved in it. Fun can boost employee morale and help drive success.

How can you create your own recipe for inspiring fun in your workplace? If you're not a natural comedian, then look for people who are and spend time with them. If you don't naturally see the lighter side of life, challenge yourself to look for it and invite others to do the same. Schedule meetings, parties, and get-togethers and let those with the gift of humor reveal themselves. And don't be afraid to ask, "What can we do to have more fun around here?" Then move out of the way and let fun take on a life of its own.

✓ Don't take yourself too seriously: People want leaders with whom they can identify—leaders who express a full range of emotions. The leader who is gutsy enough to be open creates an organization that is not only fun to work at but is also more psychologically and emotionally safe.

✓ Look for the lighter side of life: Train yourself to ask: How can I use humor to improve this meeting, to get my point across, or to bolster my team's morale? Would lightening up this situation help? We guarantee that if, on a daily basis, you think along these lines, you will tap into your own lighter side and be a better leader for it.

Are you a member of the "walking dead"? Perhaps you've even worked among them—in organizations with no life, populated by dreary, depressed Dilbert drones. And, sadly, they have caught this contagious malaise from the lifeless, humorless, unhappy managers that run their organization. Careful not to offend anyone for fear of losing that next promotion, they tiptoe through life to ensure that they arrive at death safely. Most likely, that is not how you want to live your life, nor is it the kind of legacy you want to leave.

✓ Follow your dreams—it's more fun: Too many people in the corporate world don't pursue their dreams, and they allow their idealism to die. They're trapped on a treadmill to nowhere. If you're one of them, maybe it's time to resurrect your dreams.

Look back over the last few years and ask yourself: When did I have the most fun? When was I most excited? What was happening in both my personal and professional lives? How can I re-create that experience as I move into the future? Although we can all learn from our past experiences, we're often too busy to reflect. Yet we must make time for it if we want to figure out what we really want from life.

Remember: Your gifts, dreams, and ideals are integral aspects of who you are; if you deny them, you reject critical parts of your humanity. Acknowledge and celebrate these gifts in ways that make you and everyone around you come alive.

✓ Laugh even when you're not happy: Of course, we all have lousy days. But, no matter how bad things are, try to stay open to laughter, joy, humor, wonder, and love. Instead of bemoaning a problem, gutsy leaders find ways to turn setbacks into incentives for their next leaps. Every successful career includes a healthy dose of failure. For example, Oprah Winfrey, among the world's most successful businesswomen, produced and starred in the film *Beloved*, one of the biggest movie bombs of all time. After that failure, she dusted herself off, laughed at her disappointment, and kept moving. A few years later, she began the publication of *O*, her blockbuster magazine.

✓ Make work play: Every organization requires the completion of certain mundane tasks and routine work, which gutsy leaders are always trying to enliven. The key to this is encouraging people to express their individuality. This is how Southwest Airlines does it. Though government regulations

mandate that safety announcements be provided at the beginning of every flight, they don't specify how they are to be delivered. So Southwest's flight attendants are often moved to sing them. Other times, they load the announcements with wit, making them so funny and so much more interesting that customers actually put down their newspapers, stop talking, and pay close attention.

If you're thinking that Southwest's style is in a class of its own because its customers expect it to offer fun, which has no relevance to your "serious business" of financial services or healthcare, think again. Everyone who has ever flown knows that no business is more serious than that of airline travel. But having fun doesn't mean that you compromise your professional competence or your credibility. Our point is that they are not mutually exclusive.

Our oldest daughter, Taylor-Grace, has to have frequent, routine visits with her allergy and asthma specialist. Without a doubt, caring for her health is serious business. Still, in the midst of what would be boring visits, Taylor-Grace has fun. Dr. Nancy Ostrom never misses an opportunity to laugh and make our daughter feel special. Whether she is commenting on Taylor-Grace's green nail polish, the natural highlights in her hair, her trendy blue jeans, or the maturity in her responses, Dr. Ostrom notices everything that really matters to a 12-year-old girl. Taylor-Grace leaves her appointment having had fun.

✓ Celebrate people and inspire friendships: We
were born to sing, dance, scream, shout, laugh, cry, love, and play. These deeply rooted feelings and behaviors are life-affirming and belong in the workplace. Whether you pay tribute to a long-time employee, honor a major or minor

At Synovus, fun matters and it's the sweet result of all kinds of celebration.

achievement, or throw a holiday party, celebrate your people and allow them to bond on a note of exuberance.

Celebrations help to engender and nurture friendships among employees, which are a benefit to any company. They increase engagement and build unity, teamwork, morale, and trust. Gutsy leaders work to establish an environment in which their employees actually look forward to coming to work to see their friends.

Celebrations bring people together outside of work's routine, giving them a chance to get to know each other in an informal setting. For example, during the dog days of summer, teams at TSYS, Synovus's information-technology arm, have celebrated various days with a different theme. One barbecue lunch featured outlaw bikers on Harleys and hula dancers in grass skirts; actually, all were employees strutting their stuff. Around the Christmas holidays, Synovus hosts tree-lighting ceremonies and breakfasts with Santa. Friendships among employees' children bring bonding into the next generation. Also, let's not forget the Easter egg hunt, the book fair, the "Buddy Bass Fishing Tournament" (both of which benefit a college scholarship fund for company kids), and the "Great Gift Exchange" (which sends more than 30,000 presents to charities).

Clearly, Synovus fosters the intangible magic that can happen when people connect. Within the unity that begins to develop, people communicate in shorthand and learn to anticipate and meet one another's needs before being asked. But don't follow Synovus's style—celebrate whatever and however will work best for your business. Celebrate actions that are reflections of your culture, your values, your brand, and your cause.

✓ **Whatever you do, do it with flair and flamboyance:** Flair, style, and flamboyance are unsung business assets. Separating you from the crowd, they make you the envy of your competitors by creating an indelible image in customers' minds and hearts.

If there is nothing particularly outrageous about flying customers to their destinations, the same cannot be said about playing games at the gate, singing the safety announcements, or creating humorous ads. And fiscally conservative Southwest Airlines does all three with flair, style, and flamboyance. When Harry Quadracci arrived at work with four 18-wheelers loaded with props, costumes, and theatrical sets ready to produce a musical extravaganza, he embodied flamboyance. And at Planet Honda, the entire dealership is a stage. These companies combine their flair and style with their brilliant business sense to stand out from the crowd.

Witness the success of Starbucks, Harley-Davidson, Apple Computer, and Virgin Atlantic. When the Virgin founder and chief executive, the flamboyant Richard Branson, bought the world's largest commercial airplanes from Airbus, he painted them with this inscription: "Mine is bigger than yours." Then, when British Airways sponsored the world's largest Ferris wheel in London but couldn't resurrect it, Branson ran ads that read, "BA can't get it up!"

Do you communicate in a way that makes people stand up and take notice? Challenge your team, your advertising agency, and your marketing or public-relations department to get creative. Contact a production company that stages exciting meetings or company shows. And if the budget won't allow for something like this, pay attention to the distinctive manner of meetings you attend. Borrow and modify the ideas you like and bring new ones to your team. Celebrating doesn't have to cost a lot, and the benefits are worth it.

✓ **Rejuvenate!** Stress is a major ailment that is infecting the workplace at a rapid rate. U.S. businesses spend more than $300 billion a year on stress-related costs, such as turnover, burnout, absenteeism, and mental-health problems. A 2003 article in *USA Today* suggests that absenteeism alone is costing companies close to $800 per employee—a 30 percent jump in just two years.

What can a company do? The answer, in a word: rejuvenate. Find ways to help your people take breaks, get out of their ruts, and do something new, exciting, soothing, and stimulating.

Gutsy leaders know the importance of emphasizing this continually. Knowing they can lose their personal edge if they don't take time to refresh and recharge themselves by stepping back, taking stock, and charting the future, they work hard to create a work environment in which their employees can do the same. Friendships, family, love, laughter, wonder, and curiosity are the touchstones of that environment. Helping people maintain their physical, mental, and spiritual health should become one of your priorities. Think about the positive changes the employees at Fredric's experienced when they took advantage of Frederic Holzberger's offer to take a day off to volunteer at a charity of their choice. Harmony among one's physical, mental, and spiritual health works to keep stress at bay, where it will cause less harm to your people and your company.

> People do not quit playing because they grow old, they grow old because they quit playing.
>
> —OLIVER WENDELL HOLMES

We say, **have the guts to play,** have fun, make money, **serve others,** and **make a difference** regardless of your age.

Great Leaders
Gotta Have
GUTS!

Put fifty people in a room and ask them to identify what the world's greatest leaders have in common. We think that there's at least one common denominator that will cut across every name on the list. Guts! They had the guts to go places, try things, and make sacrifices for which others didn't dare.

The leaders we have described in this book also share that common ingredient. They are ordinary people who believe that they can make a difference and then demonstrate the guts to act on that belief. By poking a finger in the eye of business-as-usual, they have accomplished what many say can't be done—at least profitably. In a "free agent" world, these leaders have created cultures that are extra-ordinary magnets for world-class talent.

Gutsy leaders know that people matter, they care about their employees as people, not as just another kind of asset along with machine tools and building sites. They find ways to make their employees' lives better, on and off the job. They nourish a culture that calls upon all employees to behave ethically, support their co-workers, and fulfill the needs and dreams of customers—while earning a profit to support the enterprise and reward its owners. These leaders inspire their people to bring the totality of who they are—heart, mind, and spirit—to work everyday. It is reflected in the creativity of their product and service innovations. In essence, gutsy leaders are the kind of people that we love to follow, and they run the kind of companies all of us want to work for.

The gutsy leaders in these pages are not superheroes. They simply have learned to lead in a manner quite separate and distinct from the usual command-and-control model. Why do we call them "gutsy?" Because what they do goes against the grain of traditional management theory; because they are pioneers in their industries; because if they fail, they face greater disgrace and humiliation than those who fail doing the expected. Of course, with very few exceptions, they don't fail. The risks they take with their gutsy behavior are always calculated, pure in motive, and long-term.

The good news is you can examine the ideas and strategies used by these gutsy leaders just as you would any best practice and then borrow from them to fit your own circumstances. Their long-term success can be yours as well. But, don't wait for your boss or your colleagues to get gutsy. This challenge is personal. Besides, they're counting on you. If you take personal responsibility for improving the lives of others, guess what? The part of society to which you belong will change for the better, and who knows, maybe you, too, will play a small part in giving history a good swift kick.

If you want to gain the benefits of our approach, you must believe in your head, and in your heart, that people matter. The most important change must take place first in your own mind—a commitment to a new and more forthcoming attitude toward your employees and your culture. Then, you have to act on that belief, even when it's not popular or politically correct. There will always be something at stake. You can take a leap of faith into a brave new way of treating people or you can protect the status quo. But make no mistake, both are risky. The good news is that you get to decide which risk you're going to take.

We understand that none of this is simple or easy. That's why it's called "gutsy" leadership. Perhaps you should begin by asking yourself: "If I was going to be really brave today, what would I do? What would I change if I walk beyond my fear of making a mistake, being rejected, looking foolish, or being alone?" Remember, the world is changed by people who are willing to take risks. So, go blow the doors off business-as-usual. Get gutsy!

If you were to be really brave today, what would you do?

GUTS!

Acknowledgments

Our friend and colleague, John Blumberg, often quotes an executive who upon retirement told a large audience of younger executives, "We should remember, that we are drinking from wells dug by others." That piece of wisdom certainly characterizes a project of this magnitude.

Thank you to the team at Freibergs.com.

We are blessed to work with some of the most incredible people in the world. They have huge hearts, particularly with regard to serving our clients. They fill in where we are challenged, and they help us make life work. Truth be known, we couldn't do what we do without them. It doesn't matter where we go in the world, inevitably someone will go out of the way to tell us how competent, helpful, and nice our team is. Whether it was calling companies to arrange on-site visits and phone interviews, collecting research data and photographs, or managing the often chaotic revision process, this team stepped up to the plate with patience and a sense of humor despite the unbelievably short lead times we foisted upon them.

To Trish Derho, Chief Freiberg Fanatic, who is as good as it gets when it comes to building client relationships, managing multiple projects, and making things happen. We value your perspective and often wise counsel. To Kimberly Henshaw, Duchess of Details, who is the junction box for everything that happens in our fast-paced office. To Paige Ryan, Chief Numbers Nerd, who keeps the cash flowing and our financial advisers at Creative Capital Management happy. To Michelle Carter, Royal Rainmaker, who believed in us enough to leave the high-powered world of booking presidents, Nobel Prize winners, and heads of state to focus on business development for our firm. To Adam Richardson, Creative IT Guru, who single-handedly has the capacity of ten people and a solution for everything. To Michelle Thummel, Research Queen and master of manuscript details.

To Terry "Moose" Millard for showing us what it looks like to fight cancer with indefatigable optimism while keeping our clients' concerns front and center and for coining the phrase, "Hire People Who Don't Suck." To Mary Johnson who tirelessly steps in to shoulder all of the major coordination that goes with our long-term client engagements. To Rick Williams for bringing sheer competence to the design and implementation of our leadership assessments and for bringing the spirit of servant leadership to everything he does.

Thank you, Helen Rees and Wordworks, Inc.

To our literary agent, Helen Rees, for finding this project a home with a publisher who caught our vision for a different type of business book. To Donna Carpenter, CEO, Wordworks, Inc. and Maurice Coyle, co-editor with Donna, who helped bring focus to the book and structure to our often, passionate ramblings.

Thank you to the Currency Doubleday Team.

To Roger Scholl, Editorial Director, who committed Broadway Books so eagerly and enthusiastically to the success of GUTS! Roger's extraordinary editorial support and patience with delays while we worked to get the manuscript right was nothing short of heroic. He also asked the tough questions that forced us to sharpen our thinking. And thanks as well to Anne Cole, associate editor at Currency Doubleday, who offered invaluable feedback on various drafts of the manuscript; Sarah Rainone, who handled endless rounds of phone calls, mailings, and manuscript copies; Michael Palgon, Doubleday Broadway's Deputy Publisher, whose support has been unflagging; the marketing prowess of Associate Marketing Director Meredith McGinnis; and the wise counsel and tireless energy of Broadway and Currency Director of Publicity David Drake and his dedicated staff.

Thank you, Chris Fortunato.

When we asked Roger Scholl to help us make the look and feel of this book consistent with its title, he introduced us to Chris Fortunato, Chris Welch, and Tina Thompson. To the degree that we have succeeded in "blowing the doors off business-as-usual," Chris, Tina, and Chris get the credit for their superb design, artistic layout, and typesetting of the book.

Thank you, Gutsy Leaders.

The real "stars" of course are the gutsy leaders featured in this book. Each in their own way have stepped into the breach and made a positive mark in the world. We are grateful for their time and cooperation. There were a lot of other people working behind the scenes in each of these companies who also went to great lengths to ensure that we had what we needed to complete the research:

- **Ed Cooney—Bon Marché**

- **Alan Kline, Eric Wolf, Jim Gottfried, Audrey Hale, Ginny Milam, and Susan Breaux—Ernst & Young**

- Fred Holzberger, Kelly Collison, and Maria Williams—Fredric's Corporation

- Roy Spence, Karen Greer and Anne Bruno—GSD&M

- Christine Campbell Loth—Medtronic

- Susan Armenta, Scott Kaats, Ralph Rubio, and Dirk Rowe—Monarch School

- Tim Ciasulli—Planet Honda

- The late Harry Quadracci and Claire Ho—Quad/Graphics

- Jim Goodnight and John Dornan—SAS Institute

- Colleen Barrett—Southwest Airlines

- Phil Dean—Stanley Steemer

- Jimmy Blanchard, Elizabeth James, Aimee Davis, and Eric Bruner—Synovus

- Jack Lowe and Ben Houston—TDIndustries

- Bob Davis, James Middelton, Inzia Miller, Susan Pamerleau, Stuart Parker, Karen Presley, Katie Spring, David Travers, Bryan Thomas, Brad Russell, Henry "Butch" Vaccillio, and Steve Yates—USAA

- Mike Abrashoff, Jason Michal, and John Wade—USS *Benfold*

Thank you, Friends and Colleagues.

To Bill Cooney who has become a mentor and a friend. His insights have influenced how we see the world of leadership, and his example has inspired us to reach higher and do better. To Chip Bell for periodically "checking in" with his ardent support and willingness to do whatever it takes. To Peter Stark for his unwavering encouragement and tremendous sense of humor over 20 years of business. Peter has an uncanny ability to make us laugh (often at ourselves) at a gut level. To Bob and Peg Eddy for their rock-solid advice. To Steve Williams, epic mountain bike man, Jim Lance, tennis aficionado, and Liz Morrell, marathon partner and biking buddy, for providing the stress releases when the demands of writing and research became overwhelming.

Thank you, Family.

The inspiration to press beyond empty computer screens and draft after draft of manuscript revisions comes from those who believe in you. To Taylor-Grace, Aubrey Hope, and Dylan for your patience and understanding when the demands of writing encroached upon our time with you. Words can't describe the joy and meaning you bring into our lives. To Elcira and Silvia for your unselfish support and for bringing order and sanity to our home. To Judy and Louie for your encouragement and unconditional love. We are grateful for the foundation you established.

Index

About the Authors

© Tim Mantoani

Kevin and **Jackie Freiberg,** the authors of the bestselling *NUTS!*, are founders and principals in the consulting firm freibergs.com. The Freibergs speak and consult with such top companies as American Express, Eli Lilly, Ernst & Young, Federated Department Stores, Federal Express, Motorola, Progressive Insurance, and Universal Studios. They live in San Diego, California, with their three children, Taylor-Grace, Aubrey, and Dylan.

NOW IN PAPERBACK!

THE NATIONAL BESTSELLER BY THE AUTHORS OF *GUTS!*

Discover how CEO Herb Kelleher made Southwest Airlines a mile-high miracle.

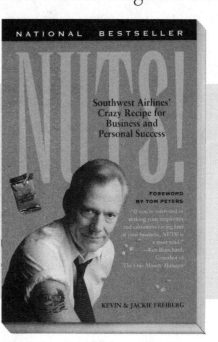

INCREDIBLE RESULTS FROM THE GREAT SOUTHWEST:

- 33 consecutively profitable years

- Ranked by *Fortune* as one of the ten best companies to work for in America

- #1 airline in terms of service and on-time performance

"If you're interested in making your employees and customers raving fans of your business, NUTS! is a must-read."

—KEN BLANCHARD, COAUTHOR OF *THE ONE MINUTE MANAGER*

"The story of Southwest Airlines is as much fun to read as it is reader friendly and useful."

—WARREN BENNIS, AUTHOR OF *ON BECOMING A LEADER*

 BROADWAY BOOKS • AVAILABLE WHEREVER BOOKS ARE SOLD
WWW.FREIBERGS.COM